WTO and South Asia

WTO and South Asia

Anshuman Gupta

Maulana Abul Kalam Azad Institute of Asian Studies, Kolkata

SHIPRA

(First Published in India in 2005)

ISBN: 978-81-7541-626-0

2012 Impression

WTO and South Asia

Published by:

SHIPRA PUBLICATIONS
LG 18-19, Pankaj Central Market
I.P. Ext., Patparganj, Delhi 110092
Ph. 22235152, 22236152
Br. Off.: 4617/18, Ansari Road, Daryaganj,
New Delhi 110002; Ph. 6594 6453, 9810522367

Email: info@shiprapublications.com
Website: www.shiprapublications.com

Preface

Proponents of the free trade paradigm must be upbeat at the victory of multilateralism over regionalism and bilateralism in the recently held Geneva Meet of WTO. It was an attempt to break the deadlock arising out in Cancun Meet owing to the dominance of disagreements over agreements on issues sought to be brought in the final agenda for negotiations. The Cancun fiasco once again derailed the process of advancing the multilateral negotiations under the World Trade Organization (WTO) initiated, with much difficulty, in the Doha Meet in 2001 after the Seattle failure in 1999. In fact, after the conclusion of the Uruguay round, the multilateral institution WTO has had a chequered history. It faced many blows, and at certain points of time, it seemed as if the institution had touched its plateau. It appeared that there was not much scope for opening up world economies under its aegis owing to many controversial issues casting their shadows over it. One of the most controversial ones was the farm subsidies—both at the production and export levels—being generously doled out by the EU, America and Japan to their farmers. In spite of promises made by these countries in the Uruguay round and subsequent occasions, these subsidies, in fact, have increased over the years. This has always been an issue of major concern for the developing and least-developed countries. While, on their part, they have either already met or are in the process of meeting all their commitments under Uruguay round of WTO, the backtracking by developed countries on their promises, especially in regard to farm sector, resulted in distrust and disappointment among poor countries having interest in farm exports. The other controversial issues included multilateral agreement on investment, trade and competition policy, trade and environment, transparency in government procurement and trade facilitation. The most controversial issue of trade and labour standards was already agreed to be dropped from the WTO agenda in the Doha Meet after concerted efforts by the developing countries.

The South Asian countries, first and foremost India, were, from the beginning, against the new round of negotiations unless the Uruguay round agreements are fully implemented by 2005. They wanted to realize the benefits of Uruguay round agreements first before committing themselves to the new agreements. However, at the initiative of developed countries, especially the EU and America, the process of new round was started. In the face of stiff resistance by the developing countries in general to a new round of negotiations and the betrayal by the developed countries in the form of not rolling back farm subsidies they substantially extend to their farmers, it was inevitable that the impasse would persist. This stalemate gave precedence to economic cooperation under regional trading blocs and bilaterally over opening up economies under the multilateral institution of WTO. Breaking the deadlock to revitalize the WTO institution was appearing to be an uphill task, if not impossible, for the time being. However, the Geneva Meet has again given a breath of life to it, thanks to the compromising positions of various interest groups. The unrealized benefits, promised by the developed countries to the developing and least-developed countries and propagated by studies carried-out by world Bank and IMF in support of Uruguay round negotiations call for a serious investigation. The present work is a modest attempt in this direction. It also critically studies the new issues sought to be brought in the final agenda for negotiations and attempts to ascertain the most appropriate position on each issue for South Asian countries.

I am deeply grateful to Maulana Abul Kalam Azad Institute of Asian Studies and its Director, Prof. Mahavir Singh for sponsoring this study. I am also thankful to Prof. Devendra Kaushik, Chairman of

Executive Council of the Institute, for animated discussions on various aspects of the subject.

Last but not the least, I thankfully acknowledge the contribution of my beloved wife, Aloka, who helped me in timely completion of the work by maintaining a conducive atmosphere at home. I likewise remain indebted to my eldest paternal uncle, Shri Laxmi Chandra, a freedom fighter, who has always been a source of great inspiration for me.

Anshuman Gupta

Contents

Introduction

The Doha Ministerial Meet of World Trade Organization (WTO) brought cheers to the proponents of free international trade, thanks to the eleventh hour agreement between a group of developing countries, led by India, and the developed countries, especially the E.U and America. There was fear lest the Doha Conference also fails like the Seattle Meet almost two years ago. The Fifth Ministerial Meet in Cancun following Doha had also met the same fate as the Seattle Meet. The reasons for both fiascos were almost the same. They were caused by dominance of disagreements over agreements among the member countries on the issues sought to be included in the final agenda for further negotiations. Just like after the Seattle failure, this time too, the Cancun fiasco put a question mark on the future of the multilateral trading system—WTO. There was a sudden impetus to increase the economic cooperation bilaterally and within region under the regional trading blocs. However, the recently held Geneva Meet tried to break the deadlock with the developed countries accepting all the demands of the developing countries, especially in regard to the agriculture sector, and agreeing to drop the sensitive issues from the final agenda for negotiations.

During the Doha Meet, members of the WTO realized the importance of increasing international trade at the multilateral level. All participants in the Doha Meet adopted a more flexible and compromising approach to reach a common point and launch a new round of trade negotiations. This was in spite of the well-known stance of India as well as its like-minded allies opposed to the new round of negotiations till the Uruguay Round agreements are completely implemented by 2005. The developed countries were very much interested this time to launch a new round on account of the on-going recession the world over. By doing so, they were ensuring the increased market access to their domestic entrepreneurs in future. The export being one of the sources of growth helps lengthen the boom phase of the business cycle, which is already at the recovery track. But the failure in Cancun had again left the beleaguered multilateral trading system in a state of uncertainty.

In fact, in the wake of the great depression of 1930s, the world had learnt through Keynes the various constituents of the effective demand determining the level of economic growth of a country. They include consumption level of an economy (C), the level of private investment (I) and the government spending (G). Later, the net export (X-M) was also added as an equally important source of the effective demand. The net export implies total exports minus total imports. This is at an individual economy level. The same logic can be extended at the world level. Thus, the international trade was recognized as a significant component of the effective demand for propelling the economic growth both at the individual country and world levels. Simultaneously, the need of international institutions to monitor the economic activities at the world level and promote the international trade was also felt. As a result of Bretton Woods Conference of the United Nations Monetary and Financial Conference in 1944, three important multilateral institutions—World Bank, International Monetary Fund (IMF) and International Trade Organization (ITO)—were proposed to be set up. Two full-fledged institutions—World Bank and IMF—finally came into being in 1945. However, the original idea of ITO could not be translated into reality, and in its place, a diluted version in the form of General Agreement on Trade and Tariff (GATT) was adopted in 1947. The works assigned to all these institutions were different, though inter-related. The World Bank was to give the financial assistance to the countries, especially the developing and least-developed ones, for the projects related to infrastructure and basic industries, whereas the task of IMF was to provide the financial assistance for meeting out the temporary deficit at the balance of payment front and monitor the exchange rates of the countries.

I. General Agreement on Trade and Tariff (GATT)

The GATT was an agreement forged with a view to fostering trade among member countries by lowering the tariff and non-tariff barriers. It was an informal institution unlike World Bank and IMF. It was to deal only with the trade of merchandise goods. Before the Uruguay Round, which was supposed to be the watershed in the history of multilateral economic cooperation under GATT/WTO, seven rounds of negotiations took place. Under these rounds, the tariff and the non-tariff barriers were brought down to promote trade among the member countries. In the Uruguay Round, the negotiations were also held on many new areas and aspects of international trade, not included earlier under GATT. These were, besides trade in textile and agriculture commodities, trade-related intellectual property rights (TRIPs), trade-related investment measures (TRIMs), trade in services and sanitary and phyto-sanitary measures.

Before the great depression of the 1930s, the international trade continued notwithstanding many wrong notions about it. Initially the Mercantilist theorists regarded the imports as a curse, as it was a drain on the foreign exchange reserve of a country and detrimental to the interests of domestic producers. In the same way, the export was regarded as a blessing for its augmenting the foreign exchange reserve of a country and giving the extra market to its domestic producers. In reality, however, it represented the half-truth. Both imports and exports are beneficial to the countries involved in trade on the basis of the comparative as well as absolute advantage theories propounded by David Ricardo and Adam Smith. By conducting trade, both the countries are better off than when they do not have it. Their economies are benefited as the customers of both the countries get cheaper goods.

The same logic can be applied at the world level too. Thus, participation in international trade is not a zero-sum game. It is rather a non-zero-sum game benefiting all the parties engaged in it. However, the benefits do not flow equitably to all the countries. If all the trade barriers are withdrawn in one stroke, the developing countries would suffer, as their economies would be swamped with the goods originating from the developed countries. This is the reason why there are more trade barriers in developing countries than in their developed counterparts. This is based on the premise of protecting the nascent industries. If one attempts to analyze the evolution of an economy, many economies would be found to undergo the following course. First, a country attempts to concentrate over those sectors where it has the maximum natural advantages, and so the agriculture sector gets the highest priority, though the basic industries and infrastructure also remain in focus. Even in the agriculture sector, the climatically best-suited crops are first developed. Thereafter, having gained the self-sufficiency in food grains, the cash crops and on their basis the agro-based industries are encouraged. It is because the raw material and market both are available domestically and these industries involve a low level technology. Then the other labour-intensive industries as textile, leather, mining, etc., are developed. They are protected with high level of tariff and non-tariff barriers owing to their being at the initial stage. By this time, the educational and technical institutions start producing the technically and managerially skilled manpower, which facilitates ushering in of the economy into the advanced stage of development. It includes the knowledge-based industries comprising pharmaceutical and IT industries, and advanced services. Along with achieving the efficiency at production level, these industries are gradually exposed to the outside competition to make them internationally competitive by withdrawing the tariff and non-tariff barriers. On the basis of the above-given stages of development of an economy, all countries have broadly been clubbed into three categories—developed, developing and least-developed countries—depending on their respective stages of advancement. The WTO recognizes this economic evolution and takes cognizance of different set of requirements for all these three categories of countries. It adopts the progressive approach as far as the rights and obligations under it are concerned—the obligations increase and rights decrease as the economy moves up the stages of evolution. The least-developed countries have either no obligations at all or they are negligible under various agreements.

II. Regionalism Versus Multilateralism

Another important aspect of international trade is that every country now-a-days is opening up its economy at three different levels—bilaterally, at regional level and at multilateral level. When two countries are bound by an agreement to conduct trade for some commodities on some preferential terms and conditions in terms of tariff and non-tariff barriers or under some unique arrangement, it is termed as bilateral trade. At regional level, many countries, preferably of a contiguous region, come together and follow the course of regional economic integration scheme through various stages of its evolution under a regional trading bloc (RTB). The WTO conducts negotiations to increase the trade among its members at the multilateral level. All these three levels work together. The former two modes are allowed under WTO itself as per Article XXIV. The ultimate aim of all these arrangements is to facilitate frictionless trade among the countries by withdrawing the tariff and non-tariff barriers. However, sometimes they affear to be contradictory. The WTO, based as it is on the sound principle of Most Favoured Nation (MFN), denies any discrimination whatsoever among its member countries, whereas a regional trading bloc allows the preferential treatment to its member countries, negating the basic principle of WTO. The proponents of RTBs, however, regard them complementary to WTO, as they are instrumental in speeding up the process of making the world economy seamless.

Another aspect relating to these various arrangements for liberalizing the international trade is its in-built bias against the developing countries. As the opening up is wider and deeper at the regional and bilateral levels than at the multilateral level, it is placing the developed countries at the advantageous position vis-à-vis the developing ones. It is mainly because of their better position of creating trade among themselves under a RTB than their developing counterparts. It is possible because the developed countries have well diversified industrial structure based on sophisticated technology and advanced services sector. It permits them to produce a range of varieties of a product through product differentiation, specialize in some of them and import the rest from the member countries. The developing countries, however, have primarily the agriculture sector, the less-advanced industrial sector involving a low level of technology and unorganized, low-valued services sector. These have little scope for product differentiation, and thus, for trade creation under a RTB. It is for this reason that a RTB involving developed countries, such as the EU, NAFTA, etc., could create much more trade among its members than a RTB among developing ones. SAARC Preferential Trade Arrangement (SAPTA), an attempt in the direction of establishing a RTB, also belongs to the latter category, thanks to its members' economic status (it has three developing and four least-developed countries). As is clear from Table 1 below, the intra-regional trade in NAFTA, EU and ASEAN was to the tune of 51.7 per cent, 55.2 per cent and 20.4 per cent respectively of their total exports to the world in 1998-99, whereas the trade creation among SAARC countries stood at 4.8 per cent of their total exports in the same year. It is so even after the lapse of over four years of the SAPTA coming into force in 1995. The trade creation in other RTBs involving the developing and least-developed countries is also dismal. It implies that the developed countries are able to meet a good part of their import needs within a bloc as a result of giving preferential treatment to the goods originating from within a bloc. It results into disadvantage for the developing countries owing to the loss of market in a strong bloc on account of trade diversion. Moreover, they are unable to create much intra-regional trade within their own regional blocs because of less complementaries among their economies. It puts the developing countries as a whole at the disadvantageous position in relation to the developed ones. It increases their trade deficit, which, in turn, worsens their Balance-of-Payment (BOP) positions. However, Article XXIV of WTO imposes two conditions on a trading bloc to minimize its negative consequences. The first condition is that trade restrictions among countries forming the bloc must be eliminated over a period, normally not exceeding 10 years. They can not be re-imposed later. The purpose of this condition is to ensure that a trading bloc is not used to merely circumvent the MFN clause.

Table 1: Exports within Regional Economic Groupings

(As the percentage of Total Exports)

Region	1980	1990	1995	1997	1998
NAFTA	33.6	41.4	46.2	49.1	51.7
EU	60.8	65.9	62.4	53.8	55.2
MERCOSUR	11.6	8.9	20.3	24.8	25.1
ASEAN	17.2	18.9	24.3	23.7	20.4
SAARC	5.2	3.2	4.4	4	5.3

Source: World Bank, World Development Indicators, 2000.

The second requirement, equally important, is that the common external tariffs levied after forming the bloc must not be higher than the average level of tariffs that existed in the member countries before the bloc was formed. It is the second requirement that is of primary interest for countries that are not members of any regional bloc. An example would make the idea more clear. Suppose there are three countries, X, Y and Z. Prior to the formation of bloc, X imposes a tariff of 15 per cent on imports originating from the other two countries, Y and Z. Likewise, Y levies the tariff of 20 per cent on imports from X and Z. X and Y now decide to form a trading bloc and impose a common external tariff on imports from Z. As per the second requirement, this common external tariff can not be higher than the weighted average of 15 per cent and 20 per cent. Although the second requirement for setting up a RTB has been expressed, in the above example, in terms of tariffs, it is equally applicable to the non-tariff barriers as well. However, with the average tariffs continually declining the old importance of tariff is no longer there, and non- tariff barriers are extremely difficult to pinpoint. It is for these reasons that the second requirement has very little operational significance. During the Uruguay round of negotiations, a suggestion to include the third condition for establishing a regional trading bloc was made. This related to the continuous acceptance of new members into the union, so that the trading blocs indeed become a stepping stone towards global free trade. However, the suggestion was turned down.

These two conditions for establishing the trading bloc leave ample scope for manipulation by the member countries of the bloc to create conditions for their own benefit at the expense of non-members. The second condition is related to the present context. As per this condition, the external tariffs set after forming bloc must not be higher than the weighted average tariffs existing in the member countries before the bloc was formed. In this way, it sets only the maximum limit of the weighted average common external tariffs, and that too, of a fixed nature. It offers much scope for the benefits of the member countries of the bloc at the cost of non-member countries.

The second condition only talks about a customs union, where each member country of a bloc uses common external customs tariffs and goods are imported within a bloc at the zero rate of tariff. The common external tariffs are fixed at the starting time of a customs union. It simply means that if tariff rates are at a high level in member countries at the time of inception of the customs union, the common external tariff rates would also be high. This situation might cause a lot of trade diversion for the non-member countries. Thus, they might get marginalized in these customs unions. However, the average tariff rates in general are coming down under multilateral agreements of WTO.

Moreover, the second condition talks about only common weighted-average tariff rates for non-members, leaving a lot of scope for manipulation by the member countries of Customs Union through tariff peaks and tariff escalation. Tariff peaks mean keeping higher external tariffs for the items beneficial for the member countries, thereby marginalizing the non-member countries in these items. The tariff escalation implies fixing tariffs as per the stages of processing of a commodity, keeping low tariff at the early stage of processing and progressively increasing rate at every successive stage. This practice stifles the process of industrialization in the developing countries.

The second condition for establishing a RTB only takes into account the customs union, which comes generally second in the hierarchical stages of evolution of a RTB. It does not consider the first stage, which is 'Free Trade Zone'. Under this stage, a group of countries gets together and decides to remove all barriers to trade (tariffs as well as non-tariffs) among themselves. The individual country is free to decide how trade will be conducted with the countries that are not members of the bloc. For example, independent tariffs can be set with non-member countries. It also does not speak about the pre-first stage of a RTB. This is called 'Preferential Trading Arrangement'. Under this stage, the member countries identify the commodities themselves to be transacted at the preferential terms and conditions in the form of tariff and non-tariff concessions. They negotiate step-by-step, bringing progressively the increasing number of items under the ambit of concessional regime. The SPATA is the example of this stage.

The silence of Article XXIV of WTO in regard to the above-mentioned two stages of evolution of a RTB gives ample scope for manipulation by a bloc in favour of its member states. They can give very deep concessions to the member countries at these two stages without worrying about the external tariffs applicable to non-members. The second condition applies after entering into the customs union. That too is very mild in the form of maximum weighted average tariffs at the starting time of a customs union. Thus, it gives opportunities for manipulation in the forms of tariff peaks and tariff escalation to benefit member countries at the cost of non-members. The discrimination might be effected till the ultimate goal of WTO to make the world economy seamless and frictionless is attained, which seems to be unforeseeable even in the distant future.

In the above analysis, we have only taken the manipulation in favour of member countries of the bloc in regard to tariffs only. The Non-Tariff Barriers (NTBs) are other areas where similar manipulations can be effected to give more benefits to the member countries of a RTB. The Indian Ministry of Commerce convened a meeting of the industry associations including ASSOCHAM. FICCI and CII in 1999 to discuss the issue of trade diversion of the developing countries, especially India, in the strong regional blocs, like NAFTA, EU, etc. Although the Ministry did not come out with a list of specific items adversely affected due to trade diversion in these blocs, it cited textile and clothing as among the most potential items to get negatively affected in NAFTA and EU especially after the total phasing-out of the Multi-Fibre Arrangement (MFA) in 2005. It expressed its fears that India might lose its share to Mexico in the American and Canadian markets because of the tariff and non-tariff concessions received by Mexico under NAFTA. The Ministry asked the Industry Associations to prepare a comprehensive list of the items that are already being adversely impacted or which are potentially vulnerable.

Thus, the corollary of the above analysis is that the countries belonging to the strong regional trading blocs with substantial intra-bloc trade are at the advantageous position vis-à-vis the countries either belonging to weak regional blocs with insignificant intra-bloc trade or having no membership of any bloc.

After the Cancun fiasco, there is a renewed impetus to increasing economic cooperation through these groupings at the regional levels. Even during the Doha Meet of WTO, the EU announced the new preferential arrangements with the countries of Africa which have been its colonies in the past. These generous attempts of creating new preferential groupings are detrimental to the basic objective of WTO in general and to the interests of developing countries, including South Asian ones, in particular. Though the WTO has the provisions of compensating the countries suffering from the losses arising out of diversion of trade on account of such new groupings, establishing such claims requires rigorous collection of information and intensive research, generally outside the reach of poor countries.

III. The Uruguay Round of Negotiations

The final Uruguay Round draft has an agreement which established the WTO institution, with its secretariat in Geneva. The old GATT was a legal agreement with no proper institutional structure. The WTO is to administer the Uruguay Round agreements including General Agreement on Trade in Goods or GATG, General Agreement on Trade in Services or GATS, Agreement on Trade-Related Intellectual Property Rights or TRIPs and Agreement on Trade-Related Investment Measures or TRIMs. The GATG is also called GATT 1994 to differentiate it from the old GATT 1947.

The WTO has five specific functions mentioned in Article III: They include

First, the WTO 'shall facilitate the implementation, administration and operation, and further the objectives of this Agreement and of the Multilateral Trade Agreements, and shall also provide the framework for the implementation, administration and operation of the plurilateral Trade Agreements'.

Second, the WTO 'shall provide the forum for negotiations among its members concerning their multilateral trade relations in matters dealt with under the agreements in the Annexes to this Agreement'.

Third, the WTO shall 'administer the understanding on rules and procedures governing the settlement of disputes'.

Fourth, the WTO shall administer the Trade Policy Review Mechanism'

Fifth, 'with a view to achieving greater coherence in global economic policy-making, the WTO shall cooperate with the International Monetary Fund and with the International Bank for Reconstruction and Development and its affiliated agencies'.

The WTO has Ministerial Conference as the highest body comprising the representatives of all member countries. They are obliged to meet at least once every two years. It negotiates new agreements. There will also be a General Council constituted of representatives of the member countries. The General Council will carry out the functions of the Ministerial Conference. The General Council also convenes the Dispute Settlement Body (DSB) and the Trade Policy Review Body (TPRB). The GATT 1947 also had the provision for Dispute Settlement Body (DSB). However, it was not as effective as now under WTO. DSB resolves the disputes primarily through consultations. The DSB has the authority to establish panels, adopt panel and appellate reports, maintain surveillance over the implementation of rulings and recommendations and authorize suspension of concessions under the covered agreements. Dispute resolution under GATT 1947 did not allow appellate review. This is possible under GATT 1994, but only on issues of law. The process is not open-ended. 'Unless otherwise agreed to by the parties to the dispute, the period from the date of establishment of the panel by the DSB until the DSB considers the panel or appellate report for adoption shall as a general rule not exceed nine months where the panel report is not appealed or 12 months where the report is appealed' (Article 20). If the panel or appellate recommendations to the dispute is not implemented by the erring party within 30 days, the aggrieved party can be authorized by the DSB to take retaliatory action against the erring party. Guidelines of resorting to retaliatory measures have been provided in the WTO provisions.

Trade Policy Review Body (TPRB) reviews the trade policies of the member countries to ascertain that the member countries are adhering to their obligations under various agreements. On the experimental basis, the TPRM was introduced at the mid-term review of the Uruguay Round. It has now been made a permanent feature and a Trade Policy Review Body (TPRB) has been set up to carry out trade policy reviews. The frequency of trade policy reviews depends on the share of a member in the world trade. A country like India is required to be reviewed every six years.

Under the General Council, three separate Councils were established including Council for Trade in Goods, Council for Trade in Services, and a Council for Trade-Related Aspects of Intellectual Property Rights. Besides these three main committees, the Ministerial

Conference has the authority to create special committees. As per Article IV.7, a Committee on Trade and Development, a Committee on Budget, Finance and Administration and a Committee on Balance-of-Payments Restrictions were created. One more committee has been created on the linkage between trade and environmental issues.

Article IX.1 says that the WTO shall continue the practice of decision-making by consensus as followed under GATT 1947. Wherever such consensus is not possible, the issue would be decided through voting. At the meetings of the Ministerial Conference and the General Council, each member of the WTO shall have one vote. (The EU shall have the votes equal to the number of their member states, which are members of WTO). The decision in the Ministerial Conference and the General Council is taken by a majority of votes cast unless otherwise provided in this Agreement or in the relevant multilateral agreement.

The present work has been divided into five chapters besides the introduction. The first chapter critically studies the Uruguay round agreements and their impact on the South Asian countries. The second chapter explores the issues arising in the subsequent Ministerial Meets, including Seattle Meet, Doha Meet and Cancun Meet. It also attempts to ascertain the appropriate positions of the South Asian countries on each issue sought to be brought in the final agenda for negotiations. The third chapter analyzes the implications of China's entry into WTO for the South Asian countries in particular along with underscoring its achievements and problems on economic front in general.

In the fourth chapter, the scenario after the Cancun fiasco has been evaluated. It also tries to fix the responsibility for the failure of the Cancun Meet. The final fifth chapter contains an overall appraisal of all WTO issues arising from the Uruguay round agreements and the new items sought to be brought in the final agenda for further negotiations besides some recommendations for equitable benefits from the opening up of the economies under the aegis of WTO for the poor countries in general and South Asian countries in particular.

Two

The Uruguay Round of Negotiations

From the South Asian Countries' Perspectives

The Uruguay Round of negotiations, which started in 1986 and concluded in 1993[1], was the watershed round in the whole history of General Agreement on Trade and Tariff (GATT)/World Trade Organization (WTO). It is supposed to be so because in all rounds of negotiations before it, only the merchandise goods (except textile and clothing, and agriculture commodities) were negotiated for free trade under GATT. In this round, the canvass of coverage under Multilateral Trading System was broadened and many new areas and aspects of trade were included for negotiations. Along with trade in merchandise goods (including trade in textile and clothing, and agriculture commodities), an attempt was made to loose the shackles for trade in services through negotiations. Besides, many new aspects of trade, as Trade-Related Intellectual Property Rights (TRIPs), Trade-Related Investment Measures (TRIMs) and Sanitary and Phyto-Sanitary Measures, were also included for negotiations. An attempt was made to further formalize the GATT into a full-fledged institution. It was renamed as World Trade Organization (WTO) and a backing secretariat set up in Geneva. The Dispute Settlement Mechanism of WTO was strengthened through making the procedure more transparent and expeditious for the benefit of the aggrieved party.

The following section deals with the important agreements concluded under the Uruguay round, how they have fared so far in relation to the South Asian economies and what more can be desired to improve the positions of these countries vis-a-vis these agreements. Before analyzing the impact of each Agreement of WTO on the South Asian countries, it is worthwhile here to take a brief stock of the economic status of each country in the region.

South Asia: Similarities and Dissimilarities

The South Asian countries including India, Pakistan, Sri Lanka, Bangladesh, Bhutan, Nepal and Maldives share the common cultural ties since antiquity. Their cultural and racial similarities make the people of South Asia indistinguishable from one another. Their languages and dressing styles are similar with a little difference depending upon the climatic conditions of a particular region. The fact that the South Asian region has been the prime centre of learning in the remote past and one of the early cradles of civilization makes it a unique region with common values and moral standards. Not only a common culture and civilization, the countries of the region also share similar economic and political features, albeit Pakistan and Bhutan are aberrations. The Majority of the countries in the region have the democratic system with executive power vested in the cabinet accountable to the elected legislatures. Though Pakistan has tasted democracy, it is intermittently disrupted by the powerful junta. Presently, Pakistan has military rule with Gen. Musharraf heading it as President. Bhutan is still a monarchy. Nepal also had monarchical system till the early nineties when it finally decided to shift to democracy along with the waves of such a move in the East-European countries. India, Sri Lanka and Bangladesh have strong democratic institutions. As far as the economic indicators are concerned, the region is one of the underdeveloped regions of the world encompassing the developing (India, Pakistan and Sri Lanka) and least-developed countries (Nepal, Bhutan, Bangladesh and Maldives) with per capita income less than $500.[2] The human development indicators are dismal here with varying degrees. Sri Lanka has the best record in the region on this count. The single most important problem affecting almost all South Asian countries, except Sri Lanka, is high population growth rates. Almost one-fourth of the world population resides in the region making it one of the highest densely populated regions of the world. The high population growth rate is responsible for the slow increase in per capita income, heavy burden on natural resources and environmental degradation at all levels including land, water and air. It is also responsible for perpetuating many economic and social ills. High illiteracy and mortality rates are other problems affecting the countries of the region.[3]

The South Asian region is still dependent on agriculture as it contributes almost 25 per cent of the region's GDP, albeit the degree of dependence varies across the member countries. [4] In the year 2000, as is evident from table 2.1, agriculture made the largest contribution (38.8 per cent) in Nepal's GDP and lowest in Maldives' (9.5 per cent), though the share has come down invariably in every country's GDP over the last decade except in the case of Pakistan, where it has increased marginally from 25.6 per cent in 1991 to 26.2 per cent in 2000. The share of Indian agriculture in its GDP has also come down from 31 per cent in 1991 to 24 per cent in 2000. However, in terms of employment, agriculture still has a prominent place with over 70 per cent of the work force of the region earning their livelihood from it and its allied activities.

Table 2.1 shows that in the decade of 1990s, the contribution of the industrial sector of the region in its GDP has also come down from 27.4 per cent in 1991 to 26.6 per cent in 2000. The least-developed countries have made major strides towards industrialization[5]. The share of industry in Bangladesh's GDP has gone up from 16.9 per cent to 24.7 per cent, representing a rise of 46 per cent during the decade. Similarly, the share of industry has risen by 46.8 per cent in Nepal and by 28.6 per cent in Bhutan over the 1990s. The rise in the contribution of industry has come mostly from non-manufacturing industries, as mining, construction, electricity, gas and water supply. In relatively more industrialized economies of the region, like India, Pakistan and Sri Lanka, the industry's share in GDP has declined over the decade of

1990s. The share of industry has gone down from 28.9 to 27.1 per cent, 25.7 to 24.9 per cent and 29.2 per cent to 27.3 per cent in India, Pakistan and Sri Lanka respectively during the decade. In India and Pakistan, the share of the manufacturing sector has also declined. It is mainly because of the measures taken especially by these two countries to globalize their economies, which resulted into the closure of many small units owing to the tough competition from outside. The second important reason is the ongoing recession since 1996.

A trend of the increasing importance of services in the economies of the South Asian region has continued during the 1990s.[6] The South Asian average has gone up from 41.8 per cent in 1991 to 49 per cent in 2000 suggesting that nearly half of the national income of the region is now contributed by services. Some economies of the region are heavily dependent on services. For instance, Maldives derived 75 per cent of its income from services in 2000, which is up from 62 per cent in 1993. Nepal recorded the highest jump in the contribution of services in its GDP by 55 per cent over the decade from 26.2 per cent in 1991 to 40.5 per cent in 2000. The share of services has also risen by 20-22 per cent in Bhutan, India and Maldives. Sri Lanka (7 per cent) and Bangladesh (12 per cent) have had the moderate increase in the share of services in their GDPs. In Pakistan, the increase has been negligible.

One striking feature over the last decade in economic policies of the countries of the region has been their consensus over the more liberalized and deregulated economic regime. All economies of the region acknowledged the importance of globalization and liberalization. The orthodox import substitution policy was discarded and thrust laid upon the export promoting policies. The import duties were rationalized and brought down, and the export promoting schemes introduced. The rules governing foreign investment—both FDI and portfolio—were eased. The exchange rates were freed to be decided by the market forces and currencies made convertible on current account by relatively better off countries of the region. The industries were freed from the tentacles of the licensing system. The financial system was reformed and restructured to meet the varied demands of more vibrant entrepreneurs

Table 2.1: Sectoral Share of GDP in South Asian Countries

(In per cent)

	GDP-Mill. US$		Agriculture		Industry		Manufacturing		Services	
	1991	2000	1991	2000	1991	2000	1991	2000	1991	2000
SAARC	367836	608117	30.9	24.3	27.4	26.6	15.9	15.7	41.8	49.1
Bangladesh	31166	48772	37.5	24.3	16.9	24.7	13	14.9	45.6	51
Bhutan	242	458	45.8	32.5	25.2	32.4	9.4	11.6	29	35.1
India	277545	474189	31	24	28.9	27.1	16.1	15.9	40.1	48.9
Maldives	165	436	20.6	9.5	17.1	15.5	-	-	62.3	75
Nepal	2819	4572	59.7	38.8	14.1	20.7	6.9	9.3	26.2	40.5
Pakistan	46899	46129	25.6	26.2	25.7	24.9	17.5	15.6	48.7	48.9
Sri Lanka	9000	16661	22.3	20.6	29.2	27.3	14.8	16.4	48.5	52.1

Source: RIS based on ADB, IMF, and World Bank Data.

of the region to take the full advantage of more liberal economic regime. All these measures unleashed the high growth in the economies of the region in the mid 90s. However, the external factors, like the South-East Asian Currency Crisis in 1997 and the cyclic recession in the world since 1998, have slowed down the economic growth of the region as a whole, albeit the region had a limited adverse impact of the currency crisis. Table 2.2, given below, shows that the average growth rate of South Asia during 1994-96 was 6.9 per cent, which was up from the average of 5.8 per cent in 1980s. The average again came down to 5.6 per cent in the last years of the 20th century—1997,98,99 and 2000. The economies of the region are also having now more even sectoral composition in their GDPs. At the beginning of the decade, the least developed countries of the region were highly dependent on agriculture and had lower shares of industry and services. By the turn of 20th century, they have transformed themselves into more services oriented and industrialized nations.

Having analyzed the economic status of the region as a whole and individually of each state, the following section would analyze each agreement concluded under Uruguay round and attempt to ascertain its impact on the South Asian countries.

(1) The Agreement on Agriculture (AoA)

It is an important agreement of the Uruguay Round because for the first time an attempt was made to bring this significant sector under the ambit of free trade, though the agreement on it is not yet complete. It comes under the built-in agenda category implying continuous negotiations unless the trade in agriculture commodities, which have been protected hitherto with multiple means, becomes completely free. The idea behind freeing trade in agriculture commodities is the same as in other commodities—increasing efficiency in production through specialization and enhancing welfare of the world community. The agreement on agriculture has mainly four areas. They include commitments on market access, domestic support and export subsidies,

Table 2.2: Growth Rates of GDP in South Asian Countries

(*In per cent*)

Country	Avg. 1980s	Avg. 1991-2000	1991	92	93	Avg. 91-93	94	95	96	Avg. 94-97	97	98	99	2000	Avg. 1997-2000.
SAARC	5.8	5.5	2.5	4.7	4.7	4	7	6.8	7	6.9	4.7	6.1	5.8	5.8	5.6
Bang.	4.2	4.8	4.1	4.8	4.8	4.6	4.2	4.9	4.6	4.6	5.4	5.2	4.9	5.5	5.3
Bhutan	6.7	5.8	3.9	4.4	5	4.4	6.4	7.4	6	6.6	7.3	5.5	5.9	6.1	6.2
India	6	5.8	1.7	4.2	5	3.6	7.8	7.3	7.5	7.5	5	6.6	6.4	6	6
Mal.	8.9	7.2	7.6	6.2	6.2	6.7	6.6	7.2	8.3	7.4	7.8	8.9	8.8	4.2	7.4
Nepal	4.1	4.9	4.6	3.3	7.9	5.3	8.2	2.9	2.9	4.7	4.9	3.3	4.4	6.4	4.8
Pakistan	6.9	4.5	5.5	7.8	1.9	5.1	3.9	5.2	6.8	5.3	1.9	4.3	3.1	4.8	3.5
Sri Lanka	4.4	5.2	4.6	4.3	6.9	5.3	5.6	5.5	3.8	5	6.3	4.7	4.3	6	5.3

Source: RIS based on RIS, 1999; ADB, 2000.

the agreement on Sanitary and Phyto-sanitary measures and Ministerial Declaration on least-developed countries (LDCs).[7] The agreement on agriculture forms part of Annex 1A of the final Uruguay Round of text and has 21 articles.

Table 2.3: Variability in Growth in South Asian Countries

Country	1980s		1990s	
	Growth (%)	Coefficient of Variation	Growth (%)	Coefficient of Variation
Bangladesh	4.2	.51	4.8	.10
Bhutan	6.9	.80	5.8	.20
India	6.0	.32	5.8	.32
Maldives	8.9	.03	7.2	.20
Nepal	4.1	1.04	4.9	.41
Pakistan	6.9	.24	4.5	.43
Sri Lanka	4.4	.43	5.2	.19

Source: RIS based on RIS, 1999 and ADB data.

The trade in agriculture has been distorted over the decades mainly through three ways. The first method is to have the internal and external policies ensuring the higher prices to the domestic farmers than what would have been possible if there had been totally free trade. This can be done through domestic price support policies fixing the minimum price, which might be well above the world prices. The farmers get higher prices than the ones prevailing in the world market. The other policies are tariffs, quotas, import licensing, canalization, export enhancement programmes and price stabilization measures.

The second way of subsidizing the farmers might be through supplying them the inputs below the prevailing prices in the domestic market or through cross-subsidization implying charging the price for an input lower than the cost of production from farmers and recouping the loss from the other set of consumers by charging higher prices. There are many example of this type of subsidization to farmers. For example, electricity, water, credit, insurance schemes, etc. are provided to the farmers at the subsidized rates. Thus, the cost of subsidies is either borne by the government alone or shifted (whole or some part) to other set of consumers through cross-subsidization. The third way of subsidization is through direct cash payments to the cultivators.

All the three ways discussed above lead to distortion in trade, which has been decided to be done away with under the agreement. For this purpose, all the measures aiming at subsidizing farmers need to be quantified and aggregated. In this regard, the Uruguay Round gave the concept of the Aggregate Measurement of Support (AMS). The AMS is calculated at two levels—product level and general level. The product-level calculation of AMS is product—specific aggregating all sorts of subsidies given to a particular product, whereas the general level AMS is related to non-product-specific subsidies. Some subsidies are exempted from inclusion into AMS. Subsidies would include both budgetary outlays and revenue foregone by governments or their agents. Support at both the national and sub-national levels shall be included. Specific agricultural levies and fees paid by the producers shall be deducted from AMS. The method of calculating AMS is mentioned in Annex 3 to the agriculture text. The base period for calculation of AMS is 1986-89.

Not all the domestic measures need to be included in the calculation of AMS. Some exemptions are listed in the Annex 2 of the agreements text. These are the green box policies that have been exempted from inclusion in the calculation of AMS for their little contribution in trade distortion. Thus, some general services, which offer benefits to the agriculture or the rural community in general are exempted. These include agricultural research, pest and disease control, training services, marketing and promotion services and infrastructural services, etc.

After the calculation of AMS, both at the product and general levels, the member countries are supposed to reduce these AMSs (if they are above the permitted level) over the time frames set in the agreement both for the developed and developing countries. The permitted level for both types of AMS is 5 per cent of the total value of agricultural production and total value of a particular product in cases of non-specific AMS and product-specific AMS respectively for the developed countries as per Article 6.4(a). For the developing countries, the limit is 10 per cent for both types of AMS as per Article 6.4(b). The higher AMS (both product-specific and non-product-specific) above the permitted level have to be brought down by 20 per cent over a period of six years, beginning in 1995, in case of the developed countries as per article 1(f). However, the developing countries have to reduce the domestic support by 13.3 per cent in the longer time frame of 10 years. The least developed countries are not required to undertake reduction commitment as per Article 15.2.

Apart from these domestic commitments, the member countries were required to bind and reduce their tariffs, give other market access commitments and reduce export subsidies. The budgetary outlays on export subsidies must be brought down by 36 per cent and the volume of agricultural exports that receive such subsidies must be brought down by 21 per cent over a period of 6 years in case of the developed countries. However, in case of the developing countries the budgetary outlays on export subsidies must be brought down by 24 per cent and the volume of exports that receive subsidies must be brought down by 14 per cent in the time frame of 10 years. LDCs have no reduction commitments in this regard too. The benchmark for all these reductions is 1986-90.

There is also the requirement for reduction in tariffs. However, before doing it, there is a need for the tariffication of all non-tariff barriers including quantitative import restrictions, variable import levies, minimum import prices, discretionary import licensing, non-tariff measures maintained through state trading enterprises, voluntary export restraints, etc. After the tariffication of all non-tariff barriers relating to each product and adding them to the existing level of tariff for respective product, the developed countries are required to reduce these tariffs by an average of 36 per cent over a period of six years. The developing countries need to reduce tariffs by an average of 24 per cent over a period of ten years. Minimum tariff reduction of 15 per cent is required for each tariff line in case of developed countries, whereas in case of developing countries, the minimum tariff reduction for each tariff line is 10 per cent. The LDCs are exempted from the tariff reduction. Not only is the reduction in tariffs by the member countries required, but also they are needed to bind their tariffs for 100 per cent tariff lines relating to agriculture commodities. There is a difference in reducing the tariff and binding the tariff. If a member gives the binding commitment for a tariff line under WTO, it can not scale up the tariff above the binding level for that tariff line. It is a permanent commitment, except in case of a sudden surge of import of that product. In this case, you can resort to safeguard measures. However, the reduction of tariff implies no permanent commitment on the part of a member country. It can again increase it whenever situation warrants.

Besides these, there is also a minimum market access commitment. This means that the countries maintaining quantitative restrictions on agriculture imports must provide access for minimal imports at low customs duties. This minimal access is set at 3 per cent of domestic consumption, which would be raised to 5 per cent at the end of six years. The agreement was to come into effect from 1995.

Implications for South Asian Countries

Though the South Asian economies are primarily the agriculture economies, the share of agriculture in their GDPs is on decline, except in case of Pakistan. In 1991, the share of the agriculture sector in the total region's GDP was 31 per cent, which came down to 24 per cent in the year 2000. However, the major part of the work force of the region is still employed in this sector. Nepal had the maximum share of agriculture in its GDP (39 per cent), whereas Maldives' share of agriculture was the minimum—as less as 10 per cent—in the year 2000. In 1991, India, Bhutan, Bangladesh and Sri Lanka had the share of agriculture sector in their respective GDPs to the extent of 31 per cent, 46 per cent, 38 per cent and 22 per cent respectively, which came down to 24 per cent, 32 per cent, 24 per cent, and 20 per cent respectively in the year 2000. In case of Pakistan, the share of agriculture sector has increased from 25 per cent in 1991 to 26 per cent in 2000.[8]

The Table 2.4 shows the growth performance of the agriculture sector in the region during 1995 to 2000. Agriculture growth being highly dependent on the climatic conditions has been highly volatile. It is turning sometimes negative at the time of monsoon failure. In Bangladesh, during 1995-2000, the average growth of the agriculture sector has been 3.87 per cent with low variation as the coefficient of variation is 0.6. The growth rates significantly increased since 1998 with revival in paddy growth and the high growth of livestock and fisheries despite devastating effects of flood in 1998. In Bhutan, the agriculture growth rates have been declining since 1996. To some extent, the recent ban on exports of forestry products since 1999 may have contributed to this. The average growth rate of Bhutan during 1995-2000 was 3.37 with the coefficient of variation of 0.5.In Maldives too, the growth rate of agriculture has declined since 1998. As fishing is the main activity in the primary sector, the government is taking steps to strengthen the sector as a part of the National Development Plan. The average growth rate of the agriculture sector in Maldives during the last five years of the last decade was 2.85 per cent with 0.85 coefficient of variation. India has seen extreme fluctuation in the rate of growth of agriculture output in the past few years with negative growth in 1995 and 1997. In 1999, the agriculture growth was just 0.7 per cent and improved slightly to 0.9 per cent in 2000. The average growth rate of the Indian agriculture sector during the period under study was 2.48 with 1.8 coefficient of variation, which shows the wide fluctuation. In Pakistan, the slowdown in the agriculture growth during the late 1990s was significant, which has been a result of negative growth in all major crops. However, in 2000, agriculture growth recovered to a respectable level of 7.2 per cent on account of bumper growth of cotton and wheat crops and a good rice growth. Pakistan had the highest average growth rate in the agriculture sector in the region (5.22 per cent) with coefficient of variation being 0.80. The favourable climatic conditions in Sri Lanka have helped the country record a 4.5 per cent growth in agriculture sector in 1999 compared to 2.5 per cent recorded in 1998, with good harvest of paddy and higher growth of output in plantation sector. However, again in 2000, agriculture growth has declined to the level registered in 1998. The average growth rate of Sri Lanka's agriculture sector during the period under study was 1.87, which was the lowest in the region, with coefficient of variation being 1.7, which shows high fluctuation in growth rates. On the whole, the South Asian region had the average growth rate of 2.91 per cent in the agriculture sector with wild variation in growth rates, as the coefficient of variation was 1.26.

Table 2.4: Growth in Agriculture Sector in South Asian Countries in 1995-2000

	1995	96	97	98	99	2000	Avg.	Coefficient of Variation
South Asia	.2	8.9	-.8	5.7	1.3	2.2	2.91	1.26
Bangladesh	–.3	3.1	6	3.2	4.8	6.4	3.87	.6
Bhutan	4	6.4	3.1	1.3	3	2.4	3.37	.5
India	–.9	9.6	–1.9	6.5	.7	.9	2.48	1.8
Maldives	1.6	1.9	1.3	7.3	4	1	2.85	.85
Nepal	–.3	4.4	4.1	1	2.7	5	2.82	.74
Pakistan	6.6	11.7	.1	3.8	1.9	7.2	5.22	.80
Sri Lanka	3.3	–4.4	3	2.5	4.5	2.5	1.87	1.7

Source: ADB Data.

The agriculture sector of the region is plagued with many ills. The region's agriculture sector is stifled by export control and regulations like export quotas and minimum export prices. There is canalization of exports and imports, though India has dismantled the canalization for exports and imports recently. There are levies and taxes. There are strict restrictions on the interstate movements of agriculture goods. The future trading in this sector is very selective. Taxes are very high on the capital goods and packaging. In the food processing sector, inadequate infrastructure and the lack of processing and refrigeration facilities are constraints. The land ceiling act does not permit exploitation of economies of scale through mechanization. The uses of modern seeds, fertilizers and pesticides are not adequate resulting in the far lower productivity in the agriculture sector of the region than the world standards. The institutionalized credit facilities do not reach the major chunk of farmers of the region. It results into major reliance by region's farmers on the traditional channels of credit, which is available at exorbitant rates of interest. These practices render the whole agriculture activities in the region economically unviable as the cost of production of farm products becomes very high, and the farmers end up with neck-deep debt trap. Though India, Pakistan, Bangladesh and Sri Lanka have made major strides in providing their farmers with institutionalized credits, they have still to go a long way before completely doing away with traditional channels of credit. The storage facilities are inadequate in the economies of the region. This results in a lot of wastage of food-grains and the selling of the products by the farmers at depressed prices at the time of harvest of crops. Another problem of these countries is the stagnant and lower productivity in almost all agriculture commodities as compared to world standards. It results in lower per capita food availability at the backdrop of rapidly increasing population of the region. The allocation for research and development (R&D) in the agriculture sector is, on the contrary, declining in the region. It is, indeed, a worrying feature in view of the changed environment for development of new technologies for agriculture and more stringent IPR regime. Unlike earlier, when the new varieties of seeds and fertilizers were invented through government funded institutes, now the new varieties are being discovered by the private companies the world over. This trend is conspicuously missing in the South Asian region.

The above mentioned ills are the major bottlenecks for the agriculture sector of the region coming in the way of fully exploiting the agreement on agriculture of WTO. If these shortcomings are done away with, the South Asian region can emerge as one of the major beneficiaries of this agreement. Though, at present, the agriculture commodities make the major part of their export baskets, the region is not a major player in this area if compared to the CAIRNS group comprising the agriculture exporting developed and developing countries. The agriculture sector has not seen major reforms here in spite of all countries of the region undertaking radical reforms in the industrial and financial sectors. India, Pakistan, Bangladesh and Sri Lanka are the most prospective countries of the region for taking advantage of this agreement. The most promising commodities include jute in case of Bangladesh, tea for Sri Lanka and India and rice for India and Pakistan.

One of the negative effects of the agreement might arise from the minimum access commitment provision. However, the market access stipulation only applies to countries that maintain quantitative restrictions inconsistent with GATT. As long as the countries of the region have the balance-of-payment problem, under Article XVIIIB, any quantity restriction is not inconsistent to GATT. However, India has done away with all quantity restrictions on its imports recently after its much improved position at BOP front. In case of other countries, this clause does not have any pressing threat at present.

Agreement on Textile and Clothing (ATC)

It was the second important outcome of the Uruguay Round of negotiations. First time, this important sector was attempted to be brought under the ambit of free trade regime through gradually dismantling the Multi-Fibre Agreement (MFA). Developing countries, especially the South Asian Countries, have the comparative advantage in textiles and clothing. However, hitherto, their exports of textiles and clothing have been subject to high degree of protectionist treatment. Developed countries have been following a restrictive trade regime of high tariffs and non-tariff barriers to the textile and clothing items. This was done to protect their domestic industries, which have been rendered uncompetitive mainly on the price front owing to the increased level of wages in these economies along with their economic development. Being the labour-intensive industry, the developing countries, including South Asian countries, have the comparative advantages in this industry owing to the availability of cheap labour. The developed countries had the Multi-Fibre Agreement allotting quotas to each developing countries to regulate the imports of textiles and clothing in their economies: MFA applied to 80 per cent of the world textiles and clothing exports, with around 40 participants and 100 bilateral restraint agreements. MFA quotas have, thus, led to a loss in the export earnings of developing countries. Besides this, before the Uruguay round, the tariffs on textiles and clothing averaged 18 per cent in developed countries compared to 6 per cent for other manufactured products. These tariffs also increased with the value-addition, being 1 per cent on fibres and 20 per cent on clothing.

Under the WTO Agreement on Textiles and Clothing, MFA is to be phased out in four steps within 10 years starting from January 1, 1995. In the first phase, 16 per cent of the volume has to be integrated with the mainstream of trade on 1 January 1995. In the second, third and fourth phases, 17 per cent in 1998, 18 per cent in 2002 and 49 per cent by 2005 respectively have to be freed from the Quota system.

Since the major part of the trade in textiles and clothing would be freed after 2005, the agreement is back loaded. This leaves discretion in their phase-out schedules. The agreement requires that importing countries should include at least one product from each of the four groups—tops and yarns, fabrics, made-ups textiles and clothing—to make the transition more even. The agreement also has many safeguards applicable, in the transition period, to the importing countries in case of a sudden surge in imports of items not yet integrated into the GATT framework. However, these safeguards can only be applied selectively for the maximum period of three years. ATC also provides for a reduction of 22 per cent in industrial countries' bound tariffs. This will reduce the proportion of developed countries' imports subjected to peak tariffs from 35 per cent of the pre-Uruguay round to 28 per cent.

Implications for South Asian countries

The ATC offers a great deal of potential for the South Asian countries to increase their export earnings. Given the fact that South Asian countries have substantially fulfilled their quotas under MFA, the post-MFA regime appears very promising for the region. However, the full benefits of phasing-out the MFA can be experienced after year 2005 on account of the schedule of phase-out being back-loaded. The Trade Policy Review Report of the WTO on the US has observed that 'Removal of the import quotas is to be conducted in four phases. The major part and most sensitive items have been left to the last phase.' A large number of textile and clothing products face tariffs in the range of 15 to 30 per cent in developed countries. In addition to these, the developed countries have invoked the anti-dumping provisions several times against the textiles and clothing products originating from the developing countries, including South Asian ones. At the same time, the post-MFA regime poses a threat to many countries of the region because they will have to compete freely with the rest of the world. The potential threat stems from China, which has recently regained the membership of WTO, and South-East Asian countries. The countries of the region, especially India, Pakistan, Bangladesh and Sri Lanka, would also compete among themselves after 2005. The MFA has helped many countries of the region, including Bangladesh, Nepal and Sri Lanka, develop their export-oriented garment industries by insulating them from direct competition from established producers. The made-ups textiles and clothing alone contributed 86 per cent, 31 per cent, 72 per cent, 76 per cent and 55 per cent respectively to the total export earnings of Bangladesh, India, Nepal, Pakistan and Sri Lanka. Table 2.5 shows the ten most important items in the export baskets of Bangladesh, India, Sri Lanka and Pakistan.

Table 2.5: Share of Top Ten Commodities in Exports of South Asian Countries in 1997-98

	Of Country's Total	Of Developing Countries	Of World
Bangladesh			
All commodities	100	.32	.09
Men's outwear not knitted	22.08	5.60	3.19
Under garments not knit	18.20	9.47	6.19
Women's outwear not knit	11.89	2.43	1.32
Outer garments knit non-elastic	9.74	1.94	1.10
Under garments knitted	9.32	2.61	1.48
Shell fish fresh, frozen	5.67	2.40	1.66
Textiles articles nes	3.45	1.92	1.09
Leather	2.55	1.86	.83
Jute and other textiles fibres	2.04	91.13	86.32
Other woven textile fabric	1.73	3.57	.84
India			
All Commodities	100	2.39	.65
Pearl, prec-, semi-p stone	12.90	55.88	12.08
Textile yarn	5.74	13.17	5.69
Women's outwear notknit	4.86	7.40	4.02
Cotton fabrics, woven	2.80	9.51	4.69
Medicinal, pharm products	2.73	13.48	1.05
Feeding stuff for animals	2.72	11.11	4.05
Shell fish fresh, frozen	2.62	8.27	5.72
Rice	2.61	16.06	11.26
Undergarments not kint	2.48	9.66	6.31
Textiles articles nes	2.43	10.13	5.75
Pakistan			
All Commodities	100	.6-	.16
Textile yarn	15.09	8.72	3.77
Cotton fabrics, woven	14.55	12.41	6.12
Textile articles nes	11.97	12.55	7.12
Woven man-made fib fabric	6.59	3.68	1.87
Rice	6.20	9.60	6.73
Headgear, nontextl clothing	5.08	5.58	3.66
Undergarments knitted	4.84	2.55	1.45
Men.s outwear not knit	3.90	1.86	1.06
Toys, sporting goods	3.13	1.75	.79
Outergarments knit nonelastic	2.66	1.00'	.57

	Of Country's Total	Of Developing Countries	Of World
Sri Lanka			
All commodities	100	.33	.09
Women outerwear nonknit	18.07	3.81	2.07
Tea and mate	9.25	19.28	15.64
Men's outwear not knit	8.69	2.28	1.29
Outerwear knit nonelastic	8.13	1.67	.95
Undergarments knitted	6.27	1.81	1.03
Undergarments not knit	5.18	2.78	1.82
Pearl,prec-, semi-p stone	4.12	2.46	.53
Headgear, nontextile clothing	2.60	1.57	1.03
Travel goods, hand bags etc.	2.54	1.99	1.12
Rubbers tyres, tubes etc.	2.37	2.05	.45

The Table 2.5 shows that India, Pakistan, Bangladesh and Sri Lanka have major share of textiles and clothing in their export baskets.[9] However, their respective shares in total developing countries' and total world's exports of textiles and clothing seem to be meager. To further increase the export earnings from textiles and clothing, the South Asian countries will have to enhance the competitiveness of their industries through resorting to vertical integration, exploiting economies of scale, greater specialization, incorporating innovative design and taking a stake in the global marketing networks.

India also will have to do away with inefficient indirect tax structure, manifested through excise duties and sales tax, to sharpen its competitiveness in this industry. It should be replaced with the unified value-added tax (VAT). Many a time delivery schedules are not adhered to owing to the administrative and procedural bottlenecks, and poor infrastructure. Corrective measures should be taken in this regard. At the firm level, there is a need for technological up-gradation, strategic alliance and joint ventures. Foreign Direct Investment (FDI) should be allowed in garment industry so that more of the sourcing is done from India. In fact, garment industry being reserved for small scale industries (SSIs), even FDI is not permitted in this segment. The strategic alliances with large textile manufactures in US and EU can be forged to attract large investment. The change in labour legislation is required to encourage big investment in mills. The reservation of some articles for production by handlooms, compulsory production of hank yarn by spinning mill for the handloom sector and restriction on exports of cotton yarn should be done away with. Cotton processing should be removed from the reserve items list for SSIs for attracting required investment for technological up-gradation. Investment and strategic alliances are needed to move on to higher value segments. For example, Indian exports are concentrated in low value segments, like grey or unprocessed fabrics. A move towards higher value addition with fabrics of wider length and introduction of fashion garments is required.

In case of Pakistan, there is a need to improve quality standards of all its textiles from raw cotton to finished products. Efforts have to be made at improving the quality of domestic cotton through greater R&D so as to develop superior varieties of long staple cotton. The industry should diversify its base from cotton products to synthetics to take into account the consumption pattern of the major export markets. There is a growing market for man-made fibre and products, which should be tapped by increasing the production capacity of synthetic blends. It is equally applied in case of India also. The main focus of attention should be value-addition instead of intermediate and raw products. This requires a strong and modern weaving and processing base with vertical integration of textile units. Efficient utilization of resources as well as increasing the productivity and efficiency of the industry are required.

In fact, coordination at the regional level can play an important role in increasing competitiveness of the industry. The vertical integration is possible at the regional level especially between India and Pakistan, and India and Bangladesh. Moreover, one of the characteristics of the South Asian countries' exports to outside the region is the low realization of value added. The bulk of their products are exported at a rather early stage of processing. Much of the value-addition in garments, for instance, takes place at the stage of branding and marketing. The South Asian countries should set up South Asian level mega companies—South Asian multinationals—to promote an integrated South Asian textiles sector. This approach can avoid the intense competition prevailing now-a-days among the countries of the region in the world market. They should establish the regional consortia of the South Asian exporters for taking over a few marketing chains in their lines of production in the developed countries. It would not be possible for an individual exporter or country, given the extent of resources involved in this venture.

Trade-Related Investment Measures (TRIMs)

This is one of the aspects of trade. TRIMs are not directly related to trade, but many of them have distorting effect on trade. In the Uruguay round of negotiations, those measures which have the significant distorting effect on trade have been attempted to be phased out. The TRIMs agreement is included in Annex 1 of the final Uruguay round text. It has nine articles in total. The annex spells out the measures related to trade, which have to be phased out.

Article 1 specifies that the agreement only applies to trade in goods. Article 2.1 says without prejudice to other rights and obligations under GATT 1994, no member shall 'apply any TRIM that is inconsistent with the provisions of Articles III or Article XI of GATT 1994.' Article III talking about the GATT principle of national treatment, implies that no foreign commodity would be discriminated in favour of domestic commodity. The foreign goods would be given the same treatment as the domestically produced goods. Article XI spells out the GATT principle of dismantling the quantitative restrictions. As per Article 5.1, within 90 days of entering into force of WTO agreement, the members are required to notify the Council for Trade in Goods about all existing TRIMs violating the provisions of TRIMs agreement. Article 5.2 spells out the time frames for developed countries, developing countries and least developed countries (LDCs) for withdrawing such TRIMs. Developed countries have two years to phase-out these measures, where as the developing countries and LDCs have respectively five and seven years to gradually withdraw them. As per Article 5.3, on a special request on the basis of an individual country's developmental, financial or trade needs, the transition period can be extended only for the developing and least developed countries. TRIMs introduced less than 180 days before the entering into force of WTO agreement will not benefit from the transition as per Article 5.4.

The Committee on Trade-Related Investment Measures was formed to monitor the implementation of the agreement (Article 7.1). It reports to the Council for Trade in Goods (Article 7.3). In the Annex 1, only two types of TRIMs, which have to be phased out for their trade distorting effects, are mentioned. They include local content requirements and export commitments. The other TRIMs having either no distorting effect or having insignificant effect on trade are not required to be phased out under WTO agreement. They might include local equity requirements, remittance restrictions, investment incentives, exchange controls, manufacturing limitations, prohibiting an investor from producing some goods, stipulation on technology transfer licensing requirement and domestic sales agreement stipulating that a part of the total output would be sold in the domestic market, etc.

Implications for the South Asian Countries

The TRIMs agreement has major implications for the South Asian region comprising developing countries and LDCs after its implementation. The implementation time is January 2000 for developing countries and January 2002 for LDCs, unless an individual country seeks further relaxation in the transition period. However, one more route can be used by a member country to circumvent the phasing out of TRIMs. This is included in Article 4 of TRIMs agreement stating 'A developing member country shall be free to deviate temporarily from the provisions of Article 2 to the extent and in such a manner as Article XVIII of GATT 1994, and the Understanding on the Balance-of-Payments Provisions of GATT 1994 and the Declaration on Trade Measures taken for Balance-of-Payments Purposes..... permit the member to deviate from the provisions of Article III and XI of GATT 1994.'

In fact, all TRIMs are imposed by the developing and least-developed countries for the specific purposes. They help the country concerned in its industrialization. For example, the local content requirement has the developmental dimension. It requires that a certain proportion of the total cost of output would be made from the locally produced raw materials and intermediateries. It would indeed have the positive impact on the intermediatery industries. Similarly, trade balancing requirement requires that an investor must cover all or a part of imports through exports. This can be done either through reducing imports by using the local raw materials and intermediateries or by increasing exports. In both cases, it has the developmental dimension as the foreign exchange is a precious commodity for the developing and least developed countries, and more usage of local content would promote the local industries.

In the South Asian countries, these TRIMs have played an important role in their economic advancement. In case of India, the Phased Manufacturing Programme (PMP), operative programme for local content requirement, performed a significant role in the development of ancillaries until it was phased out in 1990s. The dividend balancing requirement has also been done away with in case of all commodities. Besides these trade-distorting TRIMs, India has dismantled all its quantitative restrictions (QRs) on its imports in 2002 EXIM Policy. In the Indian case, it was warranted as it became increasingly difficult for it to take the recourse of Article 4 of the TRIMs agreement providing an escape route on the basis of precarious balance-of-payment position. India's BOP position has improved to much extent as a result of many reform programmes it implemented in 1990s. However, in case of other countries of the region, they can still resort to Article 4 of TRIMs agreement and continue with their TRIMs

Trade-Related Intellectual Property Rights (TRIPs)

This is another aspect of trade, which is not directly related to it. However, it has indirect effect on trade. Unlike all other agreements of the Uruguay Round, which seek to increase competition through liberalizing trade, this agreement works towards monopolization with giving exclusive rights to an intellectual property holder. In fact, the knowledge has been accepted as the fifth factor of production, the first four being land, entrepreneur, labour and capital. The advancement and competition has reached a level where to create differentiation in the product for existence, the knowledge plays an important role. The creator of this knowledge should get some share in the total cost of production. His share is given in the form of royalties.

There are seven types of intellectual properties acknowledged under TRIPs agreement. They include patents, trademarks, trade secrets, copyrights, industrial designs, integrated circuits and geographical indications. These seven types of intellectual properties were protected earlier also before the Uruguay round of negotiations through several treaties.[10] For patent protection, there is a Paris convention concluded in 1880 and revised many times, the last revision being at Stockholm (1967). It was further amended in 1979. 105 countries are its members, excluding India. The Berne Convention, concluded in 1886, is related to the protection of literary and artistic works. It was also revised several times, the last one being at Paris in 1971, which was further amended in 1978. Ninety countries, including India, are its members. The Rome convention, which was concluded in 1961, seeks protection of performances of performers, phonograms of producers and broadcast of broadcasting organizations. India is not the signatory to it. World Intellectual Property Organization (WIPO), which came into being in 1967, began work on a treaty to protect intellectual property for integrated circuits. A treaty in this regard was signed in Washington in 1989. India is also a signatory to this treaty. In TRIPs agreement, the references have been made from these earlier conventions. In fact, the TRIPs agreement, is an improvement over the earlier treaties.

The part III of the TRIPs agreement deals with the enforcement of laws relating to intellectual properties. There is no need for a separate intellectual property rights tribunal. The same judicial system dealing with enforcement of general laws would be handling the cases related to intellectual property rights' violations. Article 61 is important in this regard. It states, 'Members shall provide for criminal procedures and penalties to be applied at least in cases of willful trademark counterfeiting or copyright piracy on a commercial scale. Remedies available include imprisonment and or monetary fines sufficient to provide a deterrent, consistently with the level of penalties applied for crimes of a corresponding gravity. In appropriate cases, remedies available shall also include the seizure, forfeiture and destruction of the infringing goods and any materials or implements the predominant use of which has been in the commission of the offence. Members may provide for criminal procedures and penalties to be applied in other cases of infringement of intellectual property rights, in particular where they are committed willfully and on a commercial scale.' It means it is compulsory to provide criminal procedures and penalties in cases relating to willful trademark counterfeiting or copyright piracy on a commercial scale. In cases of other types of intellectual properties, it has been left to the member country concerned. In case of India, the Indian Copyrights Act of 1957 treats all forms of infringement of copyrights as offences inviting minimum of six months' imprisonment, which might extend to three years and a fine between fifty thousand to two lakh rupees. Similarly, the Indian Trade and Merchandise Marks Act of 1958 incorporates penal provisions for willful trademark counterfeiting. The other countries of the region can also make necessary legislative changes wherever necessary.

Part V of the TRIPs agreement deals with dispute prevention and settlement. The usual mechanism of dispute settlement will apply to the intellectual property rights' disputes as per article 64.1. Part VII of the agreement is on institutional arrangements and setting up a Council for TRIPs to monitor the agreement.

Part VI of the agreement spells out the transitional arrangements. Article 65.1 states, 'Subject to the provisions of paragraphs 2, 3, and 4, no member shall be obliged to apply the provisions of this Agreement before the expiry of a general period of one year following the date of entry into force of the WTO agreement.' It means year 1996. However,

Article 65.2 gives differential treatment to the developing and Leas developed Countries and allows them to delay the application of these provisions by another four years by year 2000. The Article 65.4 further gives another 5 years in case of the developing and least-developed countries. It states 'to the extent that a developing member country is obliged by this Agreement to extend product patent protection to areas of technology not so protectable in its territory on the general date of application of this Agreement for that member, as defined in paragraph 2, it may delay the application of the provisions on product patents of section 5 of Part II to such areas of technology for an additional period of five years.' Since the patent legislation has to be changed in South Asian countries, the time period for such change is, thus, till 2005.

Patent is the most important and controversial area among all seven intellectual properties. So, here an attempt has been made to discuss at length the provisions relating to patent and their implications for the South Asian countries. As per Article 27.1, 'subjects to the provisions of paragraphs 2 and 3, patents shall be available for any inventions, whether products or processes, in all fields of technology, provided that they are new, involve an inventive step and are capable of industrial application.' Thus, there are three criteria to be satisfied for getting a patent for any invention. It must be new, there must be an inventive step so that the invention is non-obvious, and the invention must be useful for commercial and industrial application.

Article 27.3 is of special importance. It states, 'members may exclude from patentability: (a) diagnostic, therapeutic and surgical methods for the treatment of humans or animals; (b) plants and animals other than micro-organisms, and essentially biological processes for the production of plants or animals other than non-biological and microbiological processes. However, members shall provide for protection of pant varieties either by patents or by an effective *sui generis* system or by any combination thereof. The provisions of this subparagraph shall be reviewed four years after the date of entry into force of WTO Agreement.'

This article requires that micro-organisms, non-biological and microbiological processes must be patented, and plant varieties must be protected through a *sui generis* system or patents. In the South Asian countries, presently no law gives protection to life forms and plant verieties. A *sui generis* system provides protection for a plant breeder's rights (PBR). There are two international conventions (1978 and 1991) for the Protection of New Varieties of Plants, also known as the UPOV (*Union Pour Le Protection des Obtentions Vegetals*). As per UPOV 1978, a farmer can exercise the freedom to retain seeds, derived from the protected plant varieties, for his own use make even. He can limited and non-commercial exchange of seeds. However, the commercial sale and multiplication of propagating material are prohibited. The convention of 1991 has curtailed many rights of farmers and researchers and increased the rights of breeders.

India introduced the *sui generis* system of plant variety modeled on the 1978 UPOV. It protects farmers 'and researchers' rights to some extent. Under this bill, plant breeders have excusive commercial rights to any variety that is developed from germplasm. A breeder has the exclusive rights to produce, sell, market, import and export the protected seed for 15 years after the date of registration. The term of protection is 18 years for trees and vines. A breeder can license the right over the variety. These rights will also extend to varieties that are already registered under the *Seeds Act* 1966, with retrospective effect from 1984. A plant breeder will also have to reward rural communities for their contribution through National Plant Variety Protection Authority. The researchers have been granted many rights to have free and complete access to the protected material. The farmers have also been given rights to retain and exchange propagated material or seeds from the harvest.

There is a profound fear in the South Asian farming community that as a result of the implementation of this agreement, the price of the branded seeds would increase manifold. This fear is not without reason. Similarly, the patenting of microorganisms would increase the prices of fertilizers, which again have implication for agriculture. The

South Asian countries also manifested their fear of threat towards biodiversity. As these countries do not have an adequate system of registration, the wild germplasm, plant and animal varieties can be stolen and patented as inventions. Though there is a clear reference in the agreement that the patent can only be granted in case of a new invention, not in case of discoveries, there is a very thin line between the two. Even this thin line gets blurred in case of biotechnology. There have been many cases earlier whereby the stolen plant and germplasm from the developing countries by the western firms have been granted the patent. The example for citation is of W.R. Grace obtaining a patent on a neem seed derivative, 'Marogsan-O' in the United States. There are many examples of similar nature.

Patent

The TRIPs agreement has the provisions of process patent and product patent in all fields of technology. As per Article 28, 'A patent shall confer on its owner the following exclusive rights: (a) where the subject matter of a patent is a product, to prevent third parties not having the owner's consent from the acts of making, using, offering for sale, selling, or importing for these purposes that product; (b) where the subject matter of a patent is a process, to prevent third parties not having the owner's consent from the act of using the process, from the acts of: using, offering for sale, selling, or importing for these purposes at least the product obtained directly by that process. Patent owners shall also have the right to assign, or transfer by succession, the patent and to conclude licensing contracts.'

According to Article 29.1, 'Members shall require that an applicant for a patent shall disclose the invention in a manner sufficiently clear and complete for the invention to be carried out by a person skilled in the art and may require the applicant to indicate the best mode for carrying out the invention known to the inventor at the filing date or, where priority is claimed, at the priority date of the application.' As per Article 33 of the agreement, 'The term of protection available shall not end before the expiration of a period of twenty years counted from the filing date'.

Thus, an attempt has been made through this agreement to tighten the norms for protecting rights of patent holders. It has uniformly made the length of time period for the protection of a patent twenty years for all members countries. It has included both the process patent and the product patent. As per the Article 27.1 of the TRIPs agreement, the importation of a patented product is tantamount to the working of a patent. The importation of a patented product will not amount to the failure of a patent and will not give rights to a country to invoke the Compulsory Licensing provisions. Though the TRIPs agreement has the provisions for compulsory licensing, an attempt has been made to make them more stringent. As per Article 31(b), 'Where the law of a member allows for other use of the subject matter of a patent without authorization of the right holder, including use by the government or the third parties authorized by the government, the following provisions would be respected:

(a) Authorization of such use shall be considered on its individual merits;

(b) Such use may only be permitted if, prior to such use, the proposed user has made efforts to obtain authorization from the right holders on reasonable commercial terms and conditions and that such efforts have not been successful within a reasonable period of time. This requirement may be waived by a member in case of a national emergency or other circumstances of extreme urgency or in cases of public non-commercial use. In situations of national emergency or other circumstances of extreme urgency, the right holder shall, nevertheless, be notified as soon as reasonably practicable. In the case of public non-commercial use, where the government or contractor, without making a patent search, knows or has demonstrable grounds to know that a valid patent is or will be used by or for the government, the right holder shall be informed promptly.

(c) The scope and duration of such use shall be limited to the purpose for which it was authorized, and in the case of semi-conductor technology shall only be for public non-commercial use or to remedy a practice determined after judicial or administrative process to be anti-competitive.

(d) Such use shall be non-exclusive.

(e) Such use shall be non-assignable, except that part of the enterprise or goodwill which enjoys such use.

(f) Any such use shall be authorized predominately for the supply of the domestic market of the member authorizing such use.

(g) Authorization of such use shall be liable, subject to adequate protection of the legitimate interests of the persons so authorized, to be terminated if and when the circumstances which led to it cease to exist and are unlikely to recur. The competent authority shall have the authority to review, upon motivated request, the continued existence of these circumstances.

(h) The right holder shall be paid adequate remuneration in the circumstances of each case, taking into account the economic value of the authorization.

(i) The legal validity of any decision relating to the authorization of such use shall be subject to judicial review or other independent review by a distinct higher authority in that member.

(j) Any decision relating to the remuneration provided in respect of such use shall be subject to judicial review or other independent review by a distinct higher authority in that member.

(k) Members are not obliged to apply the conditions set forth in sub-paragraphs (b) and (f) where such use is permitted to remedy a practice determined after judicial or administrative process to be anti-competitive.

First of all, the importation of the patented product is not a failure of the patent now, and it would not entitle a member country to use the compulsory licensing provisions. Secondly, the compulsory licensing provisions can be used in cases of national emergency or other circumstances of extreme urgency or in cases of public non-commercial use. In other cases, they would be viewed on the individual merits and the proposed user should make efforts to obtain the authorization of patent on a reasonable commercial terms and conditions. Thirdly, in each case, the proposed user will pay an adequate remuneration to the right holder. How much payment will make adequate remuneration is a problematic issue. And the decision of remuneration is subject to judicial review or review by some higher authority. Thus, the use of the compulsory licensing provisions would be very difficult for the developing and least-developed countries, including South Asian ones.

If one attempts to compare the provisions of the Uruguay Round's TRIPs agreement and the existing patent law of India, India needs a lot to change in its patent act. In case of Indian patent act, only process patents are available for food, medicines, drugs and chemicals. India needs to change its patent act providing both product and process patents in all fields of technology. For food, medicines, drugs and chemicals, the term for protection of patent right is five years from the date of sealing of the patent or seven years from the date of patent, whichever is shorter. In case of other areas of technology, the duration for patent is fourteen years from the date of patent. However, the TRIPs agreement of the Uruguay round gives twenty years for the protection of patent right in all cases. In case of the present Indian law, the importation of a patented product is tentamount to the failure of a patent inviting compulsory licensing provisions, whereas the TRIPs agreement allows the importation of a patented product. Thus, for the reason of importing a patented product, no country can resort to the provisions of compulsory licensing. The other provisions of the compulsory licensing have also been strengthened, as have been seen earlier.

As per Article 70.8, 'Where a member does not make available as of the date of entry into force of the WTO Agreement on patent protection for pharmaceutical and agricultural chemical products commensurate with its obligations under Article 27, that member shall (a) provide as from the date of entry into fore of the WTO Agreements a means by which applications for patents for such inventions can be filed; (b) apply to these applications, as of the date of application of this Agreement, the criteria for patentability as laid down in this Agreement as if those criteria were being applied on the date of filing in that member or, where priority is available and claimed, the priority date of the application; and (c) provide patent protection in accordance with this Agreement as from the grant of the patent and for the remainder of the patent term, counted from the filing date... for those of these applications that meet the criteria for protection referred to in subparagraph (b). 'According to Article 70.9, 'Where a product is the subject of a patent application in a Member in accordance with paragraph 8(a), exclusive marketing rights shall be granted for a period of five years after obtaining marketing approval in that member or until a product patent is granted or rejected in that member, whichever period is shorter, provided that, subsequent to the entry into force of the WTO Agreement, a patent application has been filed and a patent granted for that product in another member and marketing approval obtained in such other member'.

Thus, providing the transitional period till 2005 in case of a country following process patent is an illusion. That country will have to provide the exclusive marketing rights to the new products' owners even in the transitional period. However, there are two conditions to be satisfied by the new products' owners for getting the exclusive marketing rights. They include that the same product must have got the patent right in some other member country, and the marketing rights have been conferred upon the product's owner in that member country. These conditions are not very stringent. Thus, the new patent provisions are virtually applicable from the date of entry into force of the WTO Agreement; 1st, January 1995. India brought an ordinance on 31st, 1994 changing its patent laws and giving the exclusive marketing rights. The other countries of the region also changed their respective patent laws for providing exclusive marketing rights.

The TRIPs agreement has invited the flak from the South Asian countries for its negative implications especially for the agriculture sector and the pharmaceutical industry. The perceived fears regarding the agriculture sector have already been analyzed. The scenario in the pharmaceutical industry would be analyzed here. There is a fear that prices of the drugs would increase manifold once the TRIPs agreement is adopted in totality. The fear is not without bases. Hitherto, the relatively poor countries of the region including Nepal, Bhutan, Bangladesh and Maldives used to import the cheap medicines from India, which was having the process patent in this area. The process paten gave scope to the Indian companies to copy the new patented drugs with a little change in the process. Thus, through this route, the new drugs could be produced at the cheaper prices, whereas to develop a new original drug involves the cost of at least US$ 150 million. Thus after 2005, this cheap route to the South Asian countries would not be available any more. Even till 2005 also, it would be difficult to use the process patent in India because of the exclusive marketing rights provisions. These poor countries of the region are now required to buy drugs at the international prices. Since it would be a near monopoly of the new drugs' firms, there are even chances of more increase in prices of the new patented drugs.

However, as per the list of essential drugs published by the World Health Organization (WHO), there are almost 250 essential drugs. Out of it, only 10 per cent are covered by patents. The rest are generic. Thus, there is no problem in case of essential drugs. Even in case of non-essential drugs, the product patent may encourage the competition among the companies the world over to produce the substitute of a patented drug, which will, resultantly, bring the price down. Moreover, the developing countries, including India, Brazil and South Africa, could persuade the member countries in the Doha Ministerial Meet to adopt a Declaration on TRIPs Agreement and Public Health. This Declaration provided the flexibility in the compulsory licensing provisions for public health purposes. As per the Declaration, the least developed country can import the patented drug, for which the compulsory license has been obtained, from the third country instead of producing it domestically. In fact, the least-developed countries generally does not have the productive capacity for producing the drug for which compulsory license has been received. Earlier, the Agreement warranted that such drug should be produced in that member country which has received such authorization. Moreover, under the Declaration, the national emergency situations have been attempted to be specified. They include the endemic, as malaria, AIDS, etc.

Another area in the TRIPs agreement worth analyzing is geographical indications. As per Article 22.1, 'Geographical indications are, for the purposes of this (TRIPs) Agreement, indications which identify a good as originating in the territory of a member, or a region or locality in that territory, where a given quality, reputation or other characteristics of the good is essentially attributable to its geographical origin.' As per article 22.2, 'In respect of geographical indications, Member shall provide the legal means for interested parties to prevent: the use of any means in the designation or presentation of a good that indicates or suggests that the good in question originates in a geographical area other than the true place of origin in a manner which misleads the public as to the geographical origin of the good.' According to Article 22.3,' A member shall, ex-officio if its legislation so permits or at the request of an interested party, refuse or invalidate the registration of a trademark which contains or consists of a geographical indication with respect to goods not originating in the territory indicated, if use of the indication in the trademark for such goods in that member is of such a nature as to mislead the public as to the true place of origin.' The geographical indication originally covered only wines and spirits. However, the Doha Declaration also extended the scope of geographical indications to other areas, which are of interest of South Asian countries. Basmati rice and Darjeeling tea are the two obvious examples of geographical indications belonging to the South Asia region.

As the comprehensive IPR regime, including product patent system, rigorous copyright-enforcement framework and other forms of intellectual property protection laws, is all set to come into force after

2005, it is advised to the South Asian countries to prepare the long-term strategy in this field. In this context, one important measure would be to strengthen our institutional mechanism for patent registration, copyright protection and legal process of dispute settlement. China, which has recently joined WTO, has established a facility under one roof for dealing all with all aspects of the IPR regime. In contrast to this, our patent registration system is cumbersome. Investment in research and development (R & D) in South Asia as a proportion of GDP is one of the lowest in the world. Moreover, in the region, there is little research and development activity having linkages with industrial applications. There is an urgent need to step up the investment in R&D, especially in the agriculture sector and pharmaceutical industry, by relatively advanced countries of the region. The music and entertainment industry of the region can earn a substantial amount of foreign exchange, provided our copyright regime is tightened up. The South Asian countries have not yet mapped their bio-diversity resources in a proper manner. The inventory on the profile of community knowledge is not in place. These countries have a substantial potential in bio-technology. They should scale up investment in this area to make it a leading sector of the region.

General Agreement on Trade in Services (GATS)

The Uruguay Round negotiations for for first time attempted to bring in services under the ambit of multilateral free trading system. Included as Annex 1B to the final text of the Uruguay Round agreements, GATS includes 29 articles in total. The basic idea of the agreement is to' establish a multilateral framework of principles and rules for trade in services with a view to the expansion of such trade under conditions of transparency and progressive liberalization and as a means of promoting the economic growth of all trading partners and the development of developing countries.'

GATS approaches liberalization in services progressively. As per article 1.2, all services were divided broadly in four categories according to their modes of supply. The article 1.2 defines the trade in services as 'the supply of a service

(a) from the territory of one member into the territory of any other member;
(b) in the territory of one Member to the service consumer of any other member;
(c) by a service supplier of one member, through commercial presence in the territory of any other member;
(d) by a service supplier of one Member, through presence of natural persons of a member in the territory of any other Member.

'Thus, four modes of supply of services were recognized for trade. The mode 1 includes cross-border supply of services. The example of it is the backup offices being provided by many Indian companies to multinational companies abroad. The mode 2 is of consumption abroad type, which is related to tourism. The services of Mode 3 are supplied through commercial presence abroad and include banking and insurance services. The services under final mode 4 are supplied through movement of natural persons. In fact, the modes 4 and 2 are of prime importance for the South Asian countries. Here also the guiding principles would be the most favoured nation (MFN) status and national treatment. However, the members are allowed to give exemptions to the MFN principle and national treatment. These exemptions are subject to the review after five years of the implementation of the agreement and can not continue beyond ten years. The member countries would make negotiations on a bilateral basis. Each such national schedule spells out the initial market access commitments and limitations that might be placed on market access or national treatment. For example, a foreign bank can be allowed to operate in the domestic territory in a national schedule with the limitations on the number of branches, prudential norms or foreign equity participation. Limitations on national treatment could relate to special subsidy or tax treatment granted to

Table 2.6: Summary of Commodities under GATS Made by countries By Modes of Supply

(Percentage of commitments on service activities)

Country group	Cross border			Consumption Abroad			commercial presence			Natural Persons		
	No limits	Limits	Unbound	No limits	Limits	Unbound	No limits	Limits	unbound	No limits	Limits	Unbound
Total	56	10	34	80	8	13	30	66	4	2	92	6
Developed	65	11	25	87	12	2	39	60	1	0	100	0
Developing	44	10	46	70	2	28	20	75	5	5	81	14
Transition	52	11	37	79	11	10	37	61	12	0	99	1
Total	63	4	33	83	2	15	11	83	6	30	61	9
Developed	70	5	25	95	3	2	0	97	3	17	83	1
Developing	52	3	45	66	1	33	28	63	9	45	34	21
Transition	70	3	27	93	3	4	0	88	12	51	48	1

Source: RIS based on TWO, 1999.

domestic suppliers, differential capital requirements and special operational limits applying only to operations of foreign suppliers. As per Article XIX.1, 'There will be successive rounds of negotiations on these specific market access commitments, the first being held not later than 1 January 2000.'

As per article VI.2 " Each member shall maintain or institute as soon as practicable judicial, arbitral, or administrative tribunals or procedures, which provide, at the request of the affected service supplier, for the prompt review of, and where justified, appropriate remedies for, administrative decisions affecting trade in services'. Article XI.1 states that 'a Member shall not apply restrictions on international transfers and payments for current transactions relating to its specific commitments.' Simultaneously, Article XI.2 reads as 'A Member shall not impose restrictions on any capital transactions inconsistently with its specific commitments regarding such transactions.' However, as per article XII.1 'in the event of serious balance-of-payment and external financial difficulties or threat thereof, a Member may adopt or maintain restrictions on trade in services on which it has undertaken specific commitments, including on payments and transfers for transactions related to such commitments.' Further the article XII.2 states' These restrictions:

(a) shall not discriminate among members;
(b) shall be consistent with the Articles of Agreement of the International Monetary Fund;
(c) shall avoid unnecessary damage to the commercial, economic and financial interests of any other Member;
(d) shall not exceed those necessary to deal with the circumstances;
(e) shall be temporary and be phased out progressively as the situation improves.'

These restrictions on the current and capital accounts have to be notified to the General Council. The periodical review will be held to assess the situation at the balance-of-payment front. The Article XII.1

is favourable for the South Asian countries as most of the countries of the region are not comfortable at BOP front. A Council for Trade in Services was set up under Article XXIV. In case of services also, the usual dispute settlement provisions will apply.

As Article XIX of the Agreement mandates successive rounds of negotiations beginning in 2000, the negotiations are underway. The Doha Declaration provides for continuation of these negotiations. Table 2.6 provides the summary of commitments under GATS made by countries as per modes of supply.

The table above shows that the developed countries have not made any significant commitments in areas relevant to the developing countries. For example, in case of movement of natural persons, developed countries have made the least commitments with no limitation. Whatever commitments have been promised, the maximum of them are with limitations. Developing countries have made substantial binding commitments under GATS with respect to many services. They have taken commitments even in areas where they do not have much experience. For example, they have undertaken a higher share of full bindings under the cross-border and commercial presence modes of supply. The potentially exportable services from developing countries have not got the fair share in developed countries. Besides, they confront the anti-competitive situations, restrictive business practices, subsidies and other barriers.

Since the negotiations under GATS are an on-going process, the South Asian countries should make a comprehensive strategy to win more commitments from the developed countries in the areas relevant to them. They should seek higher commitments from developed countries in mode 4. The higher level of commitments can be secured on the basis of: rules that are transparent; no additional tariff/ tax or other regulatory restrictions on the nationals of foreign countries that do not apply to one's nationals; no quantity limits on temporary movement of natural persons, fees/ charges applicable for providing social safety nets should not apply to temporary movement of natural persons. The immigration/visa policies should be made transparent. There is a need to delink visas for natural persons for trade purposes and other categories of immigrants. There is a need to list: sectors where visa for temporary movement of natural persons would be issued automatically and occupations which would be exempt from work permit/residency requirement for short periods of trade-related presence. In the spirit of Article IV.1(c) (which reads that liberalization of market access should be dominantly in sectors and modes of supply of exports relevant to developing countries), economic needs test (ENTs) should not be applied in the sectors of export interest to developing countries. For applying ENTs, there should be in general transparent and objective criteria.. The practices of subsidization, investment incentives and tied aid policies followed by the developed countries are highly distorting the trade in services. The South Asian countries, along with other developing countries should demand to remove these practices. Electronic commerce is likely to be an important area for GATS negotiations. Since the developed countries have dominance in E-commerce, they seek to apply the GATT discipline on e-commerce with an agreement on zero duty signed., The South Asian countries, along with other developing countries, should protest against this tendency. E-commerce, like distribution services as wholesale and retail sale, already included in GATS schedule, should fall under the purview of GATS discipline. The agreement of zero duty on e-commerce is detrimental to the interest of the developing and least developed countries, including the South Asian ones.

The other issues negotiated under the Uruguay Round include the anti-dumping duty and countervailing duty measures, and sanitary and phyto-sanitary measures. The anti-dumping duty and countervailing duty measures prevent the member countries from generating the trade distorting effects. The anti-dumping measures discipline the members through preventing them from selling their products in the foreign market at a cost lower than what they are charging in their domestic market or charging below the cost of production in foreign market. The countervailing duty measures attempt to address the trade-distorting problem arising out of giving prohibited subsidies. There are well laid down provisions for seeking the redressal of grievances by the aggrieved party, though there are some problems being faced by the developing countries, including South Asian ones, regarding these provisions. The main problem, especially in respect to anti-dumping measures, is the frequent initiation of the anti-dumping process by the developed countries in products originating from the developing countries. It disrupts the supply of these commodities in their markets. In many cases, these firms are forced to close down as they can not sustain for a long time owing to lack of finance. It was one of the implementation issues in the Doha Meet. The debate on it is still on. The developing countries are demanding that a commodity, which has faced the anti-dumping investigation once, should not be subjected to the same investigation again before a reasonably long period, say two years or so.

The Sanitary and Phyto-sanitary measures of WTO try to bring about the discipline and uniformity in regard to hygienic and sanitary norms in the production process across all member countries. These measures are important especially for agriculture and food-processing industries. Phyto-sanitary measures are related to the marine products to protect the rare species.

NOTES AND REFERENCES

1. Debroy, Bebek, *Beyond the Uruguay Round: The Indian Perspective on GATT,* Response Books: New Delhi:1996, p. 39.
2. World Bank, World Bank Indicators, 1998.
3. Gupta, Anshuman, *SAARC:SAPTA to SAFTA*, Shipra Publications: New Delhi: 2002, p. 21.
4. *South Asia Development and Cooperation Report 2001/02: RIS for Non-Aligned and Developed Countries*, New Delhi, p. 63.
5. *Ibid.* p. 64.
6. *Ibid.* p. 65.
7. Debroy, Bebek,*Beyond the Uruguay Round: The Indian Perspective on GATT,* Response Books: New Delhi: 1996, pp. 91, 92.
8. *South Asia Development and Cooperation Report 2001/02: RIS for Non-Aligned and Developed Countries* New Delhi, p. 64.
9. *Ibid. p.* 87.
10. Debroy, Bebek, *Beyond the Uruguay Round: The Indian Perspective on GATT,* Response Books: New Delhi: 1996, p. 136.

Three

Doha Meet and South Asia

The Doha Meet in October 2001 was the fourth Ministerial Conference after the third in Seattle in November 1999 failed to produce any tangible results. The reason for the failure of the Seattle Meet was the inflexible positions adopted by developed and developing countries on many issues. In the aftermath of the Seattle meet, there was a renewed impetus to the process of regionalism and bilateralism in the economic cooperation. It did not augur well for the multilateral trading system—WTO. It dashed, for a short while, all the hopes many reposed in the rule-based system of WTO. The impasse was attempted to be cleared after two years fourth Ministerial Conference at Doha. Thanks to the member countries being more considerate to each other's interests this time, the final agenda for negotiations could be adopted on the limited items.

The issues figuring in the Seattle and Doha Meets were same and can be divided broadly into three categories—one, review of the existing agreements, two, agreements on Agriculture and Services (two areas of built-in agenda) and third, the new issues. The first category including the review of the existing agreements was the major subject in these meets. The working of each agreement had identified many loopholes in the existing provisions being used by many countries, especially developed countries, for their own advantages. The purpose of the review process was not to highlight new areas of negotiations but gaps in the existing provisions. The plugging of these gaps was to be made mainly through the administrative initiatives rather than negotiations.

The second part comprised further negotiations in the areas of Agriculture and Services, the built-in-agenda items. The third and final category consisted of the new issues including trade and environment, trade and labour and four Singapore issues comprising trade and investment, trade and competition policy, trade facilitation and transparency in government procurement. They were to be decided for final negotiations. Thus, the first category was mainly of reviewing the existing provisions of the various agreements concluded in the Uruguay Round and correcting the loopholes mainly through the administrative measures, whereas the last two categories were to provide the new opportunities for negotiations to the members concerned.

The Built-in-Agenda Issues

There are two built-in-agenda issues—services and agriculture. As per the consensus among the member countries of WTO, on these two issues, the agreements on which are not yet complete, further negotiations were to begin not later than January 2000. The negotiations are underway. The idea is to eventually liberalize these two important areas.

Agriculture

To streamline the agriculture sector from all trade-distorting practices, all the three areas-market access, domestic support and export subsidies—will have to be taken care of. The basic thrust of the agreement is to free this important sector from all shackles producing trade—distorting impact and bring about the efficiency in the sector through efficient allocation of resources. In the Doha Meet, the non-implementation of the UR commitments by the developed countries in respect to reducing the farm subsidies given by them in huge amounts was one of the major issues of concern for the developing countries. In fact, the subsidies given by the developed countries to their farmers in different forms have increased since the conclusion of the Uruguay round Agreement. The agriculture subsidies by OECD countries have increased from $ 235 billion a year on an average during 1986-88 to $ 266 billion during 1997-99.[1] It is roughly equivalent to 60 per cent of total world trade in agriculture and twice the value of agriculture exports from developing countries as per world Bank Report, 2001. The recent Trade Policy Review Report on the EU by the WTO has observed that "high tariffs continue to protect agriculture in the EU countries with peak on cereals, meat, dairy and poultry, sugar and tobacco. Although the average tariffs have come down, out-of-quota duties continue to protect sensitive products. The financial transfers have continued to grow and assistance is taking the form of direct payments" The Report further mentions that aspects of tariff quota administration, the use of special safeguards and export subsidies have been of concern to other WTO members.

Similarly, the WTO's Trade Policy Review Report on the US observes that "although the quantitative restrictions (QRs) on agriculture imports have been converted in tariffs and tariff quotas, above-quota tariffs remain quite high and tariff quotas are not always filled. The US has converted domestic price support to direct income support. Besides, the US grants export subsidies in relation to agricultural products under the Foreign Sales Corporations (FSC) scheme, which has been found inconsistent to WTO provisions by the Dispute Settlement Body (DSB) in a complaint lodged by the EU."[2] In additions to these, the developed countries are using the anti-dumping provisions very often, many times without any substantial reason, in respect to agricultural products coming from the developing countries. In the Doha Meet, the developing countries could succeed, though after stiff resistance, in securing the developed countries' commitments to reduce, with a view to eventually phase-out, all export subsidies, substantially reduce the domestic support and give enough market access.

The issues relevant to the South Asian countries include food security need, adequate market access of the developed countries' markets, Sanitary and Phyto-sanitary measures, administration of tariff rate quotas and dealing with the Green and Blue Boxes' subsidies. As far as the food security need of developing countries is concerned, majority of the developing countries, including the South Asian countries, have an unstable food security system. To ensure the food security, a greater flexibility should be given to them under the Special and Differential Treatment. To ensure the adequate market access to the developing countries of the developed countries' market, the high domestic support extended by the developed countries to their farmers should be reduced by a substantial level along with taking care of tariff peaks, tariff escalation and non-tariff barriers. The average formula would not be sufficient in this regard. A mechanism should be devised whereby the reduction in tariffs is effected across the board, leaving least power of manipulation in the hands of countries concerned.

Sanitary and phyto-sanitary measures are new to the South Asian countries. In fact, the developed countries are using these measures as a new form of non-tariff barrier (NTBs) to deny the market access to the suppliers from developing countries, including South Asian ones. Majority of the producers from the South Asian countries possess neither the required technical expertise nor financial resources to adopt the standards of sanitary and hygiene practiced in the developed countries. In fact, there should be a provision of fund along with technical assistance in the WTO to help the developing countries in this regard. The implementation of tariff-rate quotas should be transparent. The developed countries are trying to broaden the scope of the Green and Blue Boxes' subsidies to justify their multiple forms of subsidies. These trends should be arrested at any cost.

Services

Services were also brought for the first time in the ambit of free trade. The agreement on it is above not yet complete. Further negotiations on it started from January 2000. The developed countries have not made enough commitments in areas of interest to the developing countries—Modes 2 '(tourism) and Modes 4 (movement of natural persons)—whereas the developing countries, including the South Asian ones, have given major commitments in areas where they do not have much experience—Mode 1 and Mode 3. Besides this imbalance in commitments, the suppliers from the developing countries are being discriminated vis-a-vis the domestic suppliers in the developed countries through anti-competitive practices and subsidies.[3] There is need to make a comprehensive strategy to have more commitments from the developed countries in areas relevant to the South Asian countries besides disciplining them. The Economic needs test (ENT) should be relaxed in case of the areas of developing countries' interests.

The new issues

a) *Multilateral Agreement on Investment (MAI)*

Foreign investment is regarded as an important source of capital, a significant factor of production. Earlier the developing countries were averse to inviting foreign investment—both foreign direct investment (FDI) and portfolio investment. Many safeguards were employed by them to regulate it. In foreign investments, the portfolio investment was supposed to be a taboo, and rightly so because of its being volatile in nature. It might flee the market in no time causing an irreparable damage to the economy. The South-Asian Financial crisis has reinforced this belief. As far as the Foreign Direct Investment (FDI) is concerned, developing countries allowed it in limited sectors with many obligations on the foreign partner and ceiling caps on the foreign equity participation. They rather preferred to borrow mainly from the multilateral agencies, like World Bank and IMF, or from overseas commercial banks in case of deficit in their balance of payment accounts, which was often the case. However, the scenario seems to have changed completely as far as the FDI is concerned. The developing countries in general have discarded the orthodox approach of borrowing from the multilateral agencies as they attach the harsh conditionalities to the recipient countries, though these loans were for long duration at the soft interest rates. Instead, they have started according importance to the foreign investment, especially the FDI. Now they are vying hard among themselves to attract the FDI by extending various incentives to the prospective investors. The ceiling caps on the foreign equity participation have been almost withdrawn in many sectors of economic importance to the recipient country concerned. The obligations on the foreign joint venture, like export obligation or local content requirement, are being done away with under the TRIMs agreement. As far as the portfolio investment is concerned, the aversion is still in place, though the intensity is diluted.

In case of FDI, the equity participation is made in the form of cash, technology or managerial know how, or the combination of all three. In fact, it is good from the world's point of view also as it enhances the world welfare through allowing the entrepreneurs to combine the best and cheapest factors of production so as to provide the consumers with the quality goods and services at the lowest possible price. It is for this reason that the quantum of FDI has increased manifold over the last decade. However, it is the sovereign right of each country to decide about the sectors in which they want to invite foreign investment. Often, a country, especially the developing one, prefers FDI in those sectors where they are not efficient enough or in export-oriented areas. The unregulated flow of FDI in all sectors might damage its economy. The domestic entrepreneurs would face increased competition and might get wiped out from the domestic market owing to the financial and technological supremacy of the foreign investors coming from the developed countries over the domestic enterprises. Therefore, it is advisable for the developing countries to keep control on the inflow of investment and regulate it according to their respective specific requirements. However, the proposed multilateral agreement on investment denies this sovereign right to the member countries. It envisages to conclude a comprehensive agreement on foreign investment so as to frame uniform rules and regulations to regulate it. The main proponents of the issue are the developed countries including EU, USA, etc. It would not be out of place here to mention that an attempt to forge a similar agreement could not succeed in OECD owing to disagreement among developed countries. The developed countries want to have provisions in the agreement allowing them to invest without any restriction across the member countries in all sectors. They want pre-and post-national treatment for their enterprises.

It was one of the most contentious issues in the Seattle Meet. In the Doha Meet also, the members were divided over it. The WTO Working Group is already working on it and focusing its attention on mainly three issues, namely:

— The implications of the relationship between trade and investment for development and growth,
— The economic relationship between trade and investment and
— stocktaking and analysis of relevant existing international instruments and activities.[4]

The initiative for action in the WTO came from a group led by Canada. The other members of the group were Japan, Morocco and Peru. Brazil, Argentina, Chile, Hong Kong and Hungary had shown positive interest for signing the MAI. Malaysia, Indonesia and India, however, expressed strong resistance to the issue. They were of the opinion that any agreement on investment under WTO would subjugate their sovereignty and they would not be able to take decisions as per the needs of their respective economies. Though almost all states having realized the importance of FDI, had liberalized their rules and regulations governing foreign investments, they wanted to preserve their sovereign right for deciding the sectors and areas for such investments. In fact, they were mainly opposed to the proposed provision of the pre-establishment national treatment to the foreign investors. It would have meant sacrificing their sovereign rights regarding the decisions for such investments according to their priorities. Many developing countries were not even ready for the post-establishment national treatment provision, as it would have implied the curtailment of their sovereign rights in giving extra fiscal and monetary incentives to the domestic entrepreneurs.

Now, the position of the South Asian countries is that though the states of the region are pursuing the liberal policies for foreign investments, they are opposed to the idea of compromising their sovereignty in this regard. These countries have opened their economies in varying degrees to foreign investments as per their respective priorities. They are also discriminating between the foreign entrepreneurs and domestic ones in regard to corporate taxation, raising the capital, etc. Thus, they all were against the agreement.

In the Doha Ministerial Meet, it was decided to shelve the issue for two years until the next Ministerial Meet, where its modalities were to be decided with consensus among the member countries.[5] However, the fifth Ministerial Meet failed because of the disagreements over the issues. The reasons of failure and its implications have been discussed in the fifth chapter.

b) *Trade and Competition Policy*

The competition policy and investment policy are complementary to each other, though the competition policy encompasses trade policy also to ensure the adequate competition in the market for the benefit of the consumers. It is a well-known fact that any hindrance to the competition impairs the welfare of consumers, who constitute the major part of the society. Competition increases the efficiency in utilizing the scarce resources, reduces the production cost, promotes innovations and inventions in the economy, and encourages the better allocation of the factors of production, which, in turn, collectively enhance the welfare in the economies concerned and at the world level. The WTO is basically working on this premise.

Before adopting an appropriate approach to tackle the issue in the next Meet, it is worthwhile to analyze its implications in case a comprehensive agreement on competition is concluded. Of course, for the welfare of consumers, it is necessary to do away with all glitches coming in the way of a competitive environment. To ensure it, almost every country is either already having or is in the process of adopting a comprehensive competition policy. However, the task is not an easy one, especially when economic boundaries are getting blurred with the intensification of the process of globalization. The domestic policy can only regulate the competition of the domestic economy. In the globalized world, these domestic laws become ineffective while dealing with the MNCs, as their decisions have a great deal of impact on the domestic competitive environment. To tackle these cases, a comprehensive agreement on the competition policy at the multilateral level would go a long way. However, there are apprehensions that the agreement can be misused by the developed countries to facilitate the acceptance of Multilateral Agreement on Investment, which allows unrestricted flow of foreign investments with pre-and post-national treatment. It might also be used to make the agreement on government procurement universally accepted at the multilateral level, which is currently operating at the plurilateral level. The developing countries should make adequate preparations before participating in the next Meet. They should make sure that the adequate safeguards are incorporated in the agreement to avoid the above situation.

Undoubtedly, the competition policy is necessary for an economy. However, concluding an agreement at the multilateral level under WTO is fraught with risks, especially for the developing countries. As the member countries are at the varying stages of economic development with varying structures (in terms of size and form of organization) of the business entities, it is not advisable to implement the common competition policy simultaneously in one stroke for all the members. Rather, it is better to have an effective competition policy and law at the national level first. After a transitional period, necessary to give adequate time to domestic entrepreneurs to adjust with the competitive forces, a multilateral agreement can be forged under WTO with adequate safeguards for the developing countries.

One more issue involved with the competition policy is whether it can be applied equally to the government enterprises including natural monopolies, commercial enterprises, etc. As far as the government commercial enterprises are concerned, the competition law can be applied without prejudice. In case of natural monopolies also, endeavor should be to nurture the competition. A constant surveillance should be there to ensure that they commit no anti-competitive activities. However, often the government extends special concessions to a particular group of the society. For example, giving special preference to the small-scale industries over the large ones in terms of fiscal and monetary incentives, giving subsidies to a particular section of the society, etc., are included in this category. These measures, which are discriminatory and so anti-competitive practices, are initiated for the public good. The public good is different from the consumer good. The public good derives its connotation from the welfare state, which is the core of many countries' constitutions. It means giving special care to the underprivileged sections of the society. The SSIs are given special concessions because they are small in size and fulfill an important objective—generating more jobs for the semi-skilled workers for their being labour-intensive. The poor section is given subsidy because it can not afford necessities at the market prices. Thus, these anti-competitive practices are justified in the developing countries having a major chunk of their population below the poverty line. The developing countries should take utmost care to ensure the continuance of these practices.

In India, Monopolies and Restrictive Trade Practices Act is in place to ensure the competition in the economy. It is being made more comprehensive to deal effectively with the changed scenario in the wake of deregulation, liberalization and globalization.[6] It is being replaced with the Competition Law. The new competition policy envisages the Competition Commission vested with powers to initiate the investigation on receiving complaints and adjudicate on such cases. It is supposed to keep vigil on the practices inimical to the competitive environment.

The Singapore Ministerial Conference took the initiative and established a Working Group to study the relationship between trade and competition policy. It focused attention on the following points:[7]

— To identify relationships between the objectives, principles, scope and instruments of trade and competition policy.
— To identify relationship between trade and competition to development and economic growth.
— To review the content and application of national competition policies and laws related to trade, relevant WTO provisions and international agreements and initiatives.
— To look at the interaction of trade and competition policy:
  * the impact of anti-competitive practices of enterprises and associations on international trade,
  * the trade impact of state monopolies and regulatory policies,
  * the relationship of intellectual property rights with competition policy and of investment with competition policy, and
  * the impact of trade policy on competition.
  * To identify any other areas that merit consideration in the WTO framework.

The main supporters of the competition policy under WTO were EU and USA. Many developing countries also supported the issue as they were feeling the brunt of the anti-competitive practices by the MNCs. Many a time they had even raised the issue at UNCTAD. However, the South Asian countries, especially India, were apprehensive about the inclusion of the issue in the WTO. They were suspicious about the intention of the developed countries, as most of the MNCs belonged to these countries. They were of the opinion that under the garb of the competition policy, the developed countries were attempting to facilitate the acceptance of common investment policy under WTO.

In the Doha Meet, the issue was shelved for two years for the next Ministerial Meet in Cancun. However, the Cancun meet could not produce any result because of its failure.

c) Trade and Environment

The WTO Committee on trade and environment attempted to identify the relationship between trade measures and environmental concerns to promote sustainable economic development. The aim was to conclude an agreement on environment with linkage of environmental protection with trade measures. The concerns over the environmental protection had been raised earlier also in the GATT negotiations. Even after the Uruguay Round, the issue got its manifestations in the trade-related disputes. A large number of developing countries are of the view that developed countries are trying to impose environmental standards to restrict market access of their products in their markets. This was evident from the US action, which banned imports of shrimp and shrimp products from India. India took the matter to the WTO dispute settlement body. The WTO panel clearly indicated that the US action was a threat to the multilateral system. There are many such instances. By and large, the developing countries do not have the required infrastructure and resources to fight import bans or trade restrictions at WTO. The inclusion of environmental issue in WTO and its linkage with trade would give an extra weapon to the developed countries to use it against the developing ones. The earlier instances in trade-related disputes had amply shown it. It would be used as new non-tariff barrier.

The two issues on environment before the WTO were:

— Relationship between the WTO and the provisions of multilateral environmental agreements (MEAs), and
— Environmental objectives including establishing technical standards, packaging and labeling requirements and sanitary and phyto-sanitary restrictions.

The WTO agreements on technical barriers to trade (TBT) and sanitary and phyto-sanitary measures were already there as potential tools in the hand of developed countries to be used against the developing countries' exports. An exclusive agreement on environment was viewed by developing countries at large as yet another pretext to be used by the developed countries to deny the market access to their products. In fact, it is unjustified to expect very high standards of environmental norms from the developing countries in the face of their lack of resources. It is even more so if one considers taking into account the main culprits responsible for the deteriorating environment over the years. Recently, a study by the Times magazine indicated that the US, EU and Japan are the main contributors to global warming. In these countries the enterprises are cash-rich, they having disposed of the obsolete eco-unfriendly technologies to the third world countries and have themselves shifted to the eco-friendly technologies. Asking the poor countries in this backdrop to use the costly technologies or face restrictions to their exports is totally unjustified unless they are provided with the resource assistance. In the Doha Meet, the issue was decided to be taken up for negotiations with much dilution from its original form.

e) Trade and Labour Standards

The labour standards and its linkage with trade was the main issue responsible for the collapse of the Seattle Meet. At the Uruguay Round, the developed countries insisted for the inclusion of labour standards in the realm of GATT. The issue of trade and labour standards rests on the question of 'social dumping' mooted by the developed countries. The basic premise is that the lower wages generally prevailing in the developing countries provide increased market access to their products in the international market. This enhances their competitiveness in an unjustifiable manner. The argument advanced by the developed states was aimed at securing protection to their labour-intensive industries. Their labor-intensive industries have become uncompetitive in the course of time vis-à-vis their counterparts from developing countries owing to the increased wage levels in developed countries. Moreover, the labour standards are the function of economic advancement of a country concerned. As an economy develops its labour standards also improve. Even the developed economies of today had poor labour standards when they were at the developing stage.

There were debates at the WTO forum for and against the inclusion of "Social Clause" in the multilateral trading system. Suggestions were mooted by the developing countries to promote labour rights through positive measures such as better market access, enhanced official development assistance, educational programmes, etc. The labour standard is a social issue and should be solved either through the domestic institutions of the respective countries or through the International Labour Organization (ILO). WTO has no business whatsoever with the labour issue. It is certain that low labour standards will not necessarily lead to greater market access or vice versa. This is also the conclusion of the OECD-conducted study. Therefore, it can not be used as a tool to deny legitimate market access to any country. Moreover, denying the market access to developing countries' enterprises using the sub-standard labour norms would further deteriorate the position of these workers, as the denial of market access might lead to the closure of these firms. The issue came up for discussion at the Singapore Ministerial Conference of the WTO in 1996.[8] The developing countries were able to get the participants to agree that the ILO was the competent body to do such a work. The Singapore Declaration said that "we reject the use of labour standards for protectionist purposes and agree that the comparative advantage of the developing countries must in no way be put in question". However, at the second WTO Ministerial Conference held in Geneva in 1998, the US again indicated that the core labour standards would be an issue in the future world trade talks. At the Seattle Meet, this became the main issue for the US, as the country was to go for the presidential election just after the Meet. The same issue was mainly responsible for the Seattle failure. The debate remained inconclusive until recently when in the Doha Meet, it was decided finally that the International Labour Organization (ILO) is the right forum to take care of this social malaise.

The South Asian Countries were against the inclusion of the labour issue in the WTO right from the beginning. India was the front runner in this regard. In fact, South Asia comprises the developing and least developed countries, and so cheap labour is the main comparative advantage for it. Of course, there is no denying of the fact that there are some social ills in the form of child labour, sub-standard working conditions, lack of social security, discrimination between male and female workers, etc. However, there are enough domestic laws and institutions to tackle them. Moreover, the Non-Governmental Organizations (NGOs) are actively working to expose these social abuses and force the governments to take corrective measures.

f) Trade Facilitation

It was the most uncontroversial issue in the Seattle and Doha Meets. All members with some reservations had favored this issue. The idea was to bring in uniformity in the international marketing environment and trading procedures. The Singapore Ministerial Conference adopted a work programme on trade facilitation at the initiative of the European Union. The Goods Council of the WTO was directed to undertake exploratory and analytical work to study the work of other relevant international organizations for simplification of trade procedures in order to assess the scope of WTO provisions. The basic purpose was to harmonize the rules and procedures for the trading community. The Kyoto Convention of 1973 administered by the World Customs Organization is the first agreement in this regard adopted by around 55 countries. Among other organizations which have contributed on this issue are UNCTAD, ECE, APEC and the International Chamber of Commerce. The Business community of both developing and developed countries welcomed this initiative at the WTO.

Transparency in Government Procurement

This is one of the four Singapore issues.[9] It talks about the transparency in all government procurements along with applying the principles of most-favoured nation and national treatment. The government is the biggest buyer in almost every country—be it a developing or developed one. The proposed issue involves many serious repercussions especially for the developing countries, where many economic and welfare activities are carried out by the government. The governments in many developing countries generally buy from the domestic firms to give business to them. Or, whenever the procurement is made at the world level through tender, the domestic firms are given favour in terms of price. For example, if the difference is less than certain percentage—say 10 per cent—between the prices quoted by the foreign firm and the domestic firm, the tender would go in favour of the domestic firm. These practices are very helpful in the process of industrialization of the developing countries, as they provide the market to the not-very-efficient-domestic firms. The agreement on this issue means denial of this route of industrialization to the developing countries, including South Asian ones.

The South Asian countries were against this issue. The government works at multiple levels in a country. At the local level, the amount involved in the procurement is not big enough warranting tenders at the world level. Thus, it is more appropriate either to fix an amount above which the provisions of this agreement would apply or draw a line stating that, for example, procurements from the state and central governments would fall under the ambit of this agreement and the country concerned has the full freedom to give concessions to local firms. Because of the resistance of the developing countries in general, the issue was shelved for two years to be taken up in the Cancun meet.

NOTES AND REFERENCES

1. *South Asia Development and Cooperation Report 2001/02: RIS for Non-Aligned and Developed Countries* New Delhi, p. 15.
2. *Ibid.* p.15.
3. Ibid. p. 17.
4. Kaushik, P.D., *Millennium Round Agenda: A Global Perspective*, Rajiv Gandhi Institute for Contemporary Studies, New Delhi, 1999, p. 44.
5. *South Asia Development and Cooperation Report 2001/02: RIS for Non-Aligned and Developed Countries*, New Delhi, p. 24.
6. Pani, Narendra, Managing Competition, *The Economic Times*, October 26, 2001.
7. Kaushik, P.D., *Millennium Round Agenda: A Global Perspective*, Rajiv Gandhi Institute for Contemporary Studies, New Delhi, 1999, p. 47.
8. Pant, Manoj, 'First the Stick and Now Carrot: Labour Standards in WTO, *The Economic Times*, January 4, 2002.
9. *South Asia Development and Cooperation Report 2001/02: RIS for Non-Aligned and Developed Countries*, New Delhi, p. 24.

Four

China's Entry in WTO

Implications for South Asia

China's Miracle

China is supposed to be a miracle for its continuously accounting an average growth rate of over 10 per cent for almost one and a half decade. Even at the time of South-East Asian crisis, when the whole Asia was directly in the grip of recession and the rest of the world was indirectly feeling its brunt, China managed its economy meticulously.[1] The average economic growth rate of the world in years 1997 and 1998 was merely a little over 2 per cent, whereas China could secure a respectable growth rate of over 8 per cent during the same period. Even during the on-going world-wide recession, China could secure a rather good economic growth rate. China's economy grew at the rate of over 7 per cent during the year 2002-03. The credit should go to the unique structure of China's economy.It has two parallel economies working in tandem—one is as free as the US economy and the market forces are in full swing there, and the second is under the full command of the government. Both segments are contributing equally to the economy's GNP. The market economy of China, which mainly operates from the eastern coastal area, largely produces for the international market. The enterprises here mainly belong to foreigners, who have invested in Special Economic Zones (SEZs), whereas the controlled constituent of the economy mainly produces for the domestic consumption. This unique arrangement is basically helpful in managing the economy at the time of crisis. For example, during the recessionary phase in the wake of South-Eastern financial crisis and the on-going recession, when it was difficult to secure the economic growth from the external sector owing to the world-wide slowdown, China could achieve high growth rate through managing the economy from inside by directing the investment in the domestic economy. Faced with the problem at the external and internal fronts, China took the following measures.

China attempted to expand the domestic demand through stepping up the investment, adjusting investment structure, intensifying activities in infrastructure, such as irrigation work in rural areas, railways, highways, communications, environmental protection, urban infrastructure construction, and new hi-tech development, increasing the proportion of investment in technological transformation and quickening the pace of housing construction.[2] Along with stepping up the domestic investment, the state imposed a strict control on the industrial items that already produced more products than the market demand or produced products that were inferior in quality. In fact, the Chinese growth figure is always criticized for its being exaggerated owing to the over-production by the state-owned enterprises (SOEs) without demand in the market (domestic and international both). They only fill the inventories. The Chinese statisticians count them at the prevailing market prices while calculating the GNP. These products are then dumped at half prices. In fact, the Chinese menace of cheap imports haunting the South Asian entrepreneurs has its roots in this practice. This is the drawback of the controlled economy. The allocation of resources is not efficient. It is not so in the market economy. The market has its own automatic mechanism to channel the efficient use of resources. The government approved more than 70 large and medium scale projects with investment amounting to RMB 446.2 billion Yuan. The increasing investment in fixed assets pulled up production of the important industries such as iron and steel, cement and glass, and also promoted the demands of energy and transportation. This was the direct impact of increasing investment in fixed assets. The multiplier impact further increased the demand of other consumer durable goods, and thus the overall impact on the economic growth was to be proportionately larger than the initial amount invested in the fixed assets.

Besides increasing the domestic demand, the Chinese government tried to increase its exports through various measures. The Chinese exports account for roughly 20 per cent of its GDP. For promoting exports, China did not rely on the price factors through devaluing its Yuan in the wake major of devaluation in the currencies of the South-East Asian countries, especially Japanese Yen, with whom China has major trade relation. Rather it adopted non-price measures to promote its exports. They included simplifying the procedures for import and export, increasing export incentives, developing multi-market strategy and extending sufficient loans at the cheaper rate to the export activities. These measures helped maintain the momentum of export growth. From January to August 1999, the total volume of China's imports and exports reached US$ 205.9 billion, a 3.3 per cent increase over that of the same period last year, with trade surplus of US$ 31.38 billion, a 22.7 per cent increase over that of the same period last year. In this crisis time, China could attract a substantial amount of foreign direct investment. From January to August1999, the contracted foreign capital to China amounted to US $ 31.74 billion, a 6 per cent increase, and foreign capital actually utilized was US $ 27.42 billion, only a slight drop compared to the last year.

During the South-East Asian currency crisis, when every country, especially its trade rivals in the US and EU markets from South-East Asia, including Japan, did the downward revision of their currencies' exchange rates, China did not emulate them. China's decision was based on the premise that the devaluation of the currency increases the country's competitiveness for a short time, and its positive effect is soon neutralized by the increased inflation rate in the economy through rise in prices of imports and the competitive devaluation by the rival countries. More seriously, it could damage the confidence of foreign investors and domestic citizens in the country's exchange rate and monetary policy. It, in turn, has a dampening impact on the economic and financial environment of the country, thereby pulling down the overall growth rate of the economy. China did have such lessons in 1992 and 1993.[3] From the long-term perspective, it is always better to pay attention to the non-price factors rather than price measures like devaluation to increase the competitiveness. The competitiveness in the market economy is the function of price and quality. China laid emphasis on the product quality and technological contents of the exported products. Moreover, the price can be kept competitive through the cost effectiveness. China's commitment to maintaining its currency's stability is based on its stable macro-economic environment.

The management of the economic growth by China in the crisis time has many lessons to be taught to the developing countries in general and South Asian countries in particular. Firstly, the South Asian Countries are time and again engaged in the exchange rate war to increase the competitiveness of their products, being unmindful to its adverse impact on the economy and its short-term results. They pay little attention to the non-price factors, such as increasing productivity in the economy, improving quality, upgrading their infrastructure (especially the export infrastructure), etc.

Secondly, many South Asian countries are aggressively pursuing the programme of liberalization and privatization. In pursuit of this programme, they have relegated the position of the government enterprises in relation to the private ones. India, for instance, is recklessly selling the state-owned enterprises without devising a proper strategy for the use of the proceeds. In of china, the stepping up of the government investment in these SOEs and infrastructure projects could save the economy from experiencing a deep drop in the growth rate. It shows the importance of the SOEs in an economy. Through the SOEs and other government-owned projects, the government can have control over an economy, which would be helpful in the time of recession. This control mechanism would be missing in the absence of the SOEs. If all the economic activities are held by the private sector and the government has very little role to play, the Keynesian approach to tackle the recession would not work, as the private sector would not come forward to increase the investment when the economy is at the downward journey. So there should be a judicious mix of the private and government sectors. The proceeds acquired through selling the SOEs should be used to retire old debts of the government and establishing the other government projects especially in infrastructure and other areas best suited for the economy. Of course, there should be a clear-cut demarcation of where the government should lay its hands and the areas for the private sector.

The third lesson South Asian countries need to learn from China is making proper policies for the laid-off workers in the course of restructuring their economies. In China, the government and the relevant departments have pursued measures including extending the coverage of the unemployment insurance, raising the contribution rate of unemployment insurance premium, quickening the pace of developing service industries and private sectors in order to absorb more labour force, comprehensively managing various service centres for re-employment, taking care of the basic needs of the laid-off workers, implementing the policy to diversifying re-employment sources for the laid-off workers, promoting the employment preparation system by carrying out the job training, implementing the minimum life guarantee system for urban residents and quickening the pace of reforming the pension system and medical insurance. In India, for example, none of the above mentioned policies is in place. There are no adequate safety measures and reemployment scheme for laid-off workers in India. It results in stiff resistance from workers for any move towards privatization of SOEs besides producing instability in the society. The major retrenchment of workers in the course of restructuring the economy would cause the dampening impact on the economic growth, as the overall consumption level in the economy would decrease. So a proper attention should be paid for the reemployment and safety nets of the laid-off workers.

China Domestic Problems

China's economy is undergoing transformation ever since it started reform programmes in 1978. However, it is still afflicted with many serious problems that warrant urgent attention.

The economic efficiency of the state-owned enterprises in China is very low. Over the years, the redundancy of the construction has led to irrational industrial structure, and there is huge stockpiling of products that can not be sold in the market because of lack of demand or poor quality. Some enterprises—large and medium sized—are in the process of restructuring, upgrading or production shift to get fitted into the competitive environment. However, the recessionary forces the world over are slowing down the process. The delay in repayment of debts on the part of enterprises is increasing. The real estate problem has assumed an alarming size. Until now, there have been 70 million square meters of real estates that could not be sold on account of problems like prices and quality. For the same reasons, there is a great deal of ordinary housing lying unsold. China's economy is undergoing a restructuring process leading to a substantial laid-off of the workers in the short run. By the turn of last century, the laid-off workers in China had already touched 15 million mark. The unemployment pressure is likely to increase in the near future when the reform programmes would be deepened. Government at various levels and relevant departments are adopting a series of measures to contain the negative impact of the increasing unemployment in the economy. Besides laid-off workers on account of restructuring of the economy, there are millions of people in the country living in abject poverty. Moreover, in the next few years, there will be more surplus of labour in the rural areas, which would be forced to migrate to the urban areas for the want of seeking gainful employment. It would increase the competition for laid-off workers for the limited employment opportunities.

The financial sector is not yet developed in China. Capital market is still at the nascent stage. The equity market is not developed. The enterprises still prefer to raise the capital through bank loans. The commercial banks are still working on a non-business principles and extending loans to the enterprises without adequate precautions. This is the reason as to why the financial institutions here suffer from the problem of relatively high proportion of bad loans. The total bad loans of the financial institutions in China accounted for over 25 per cent of their total loans, which is very high in comparison to the world standards. Moreover, the illegal activities in the financial sector and operation against the relevant regulations are rampant.

There is a serious problem in the fiscal position of the state—revenue is decreasing and expenditure is under pressure. The prolonged recession, first on account of South-East Asian crisis and then current recession, has had its toll on the revenue side of the budget, whereas the pressure on expenditure side increased owing to many reasons. They included carrying out the protective policy for grain purchase, helping state-owned enterprises to cope up with their difficulties and supporting the laid–off workers besides stepping up government spending on fresh investments to infuse the necessary effective demand in the economy.

China After Joining WTO

China has successfully steered itself into WTO by concluding the bilateral negotiations with the existing member countries. China opted out of multilateral arrangement (GATT) way back in 1953. It was seeking its re-entry since 1982, and for achieving this end, it underwent a series of bilateral negotiations with the member countries. There are clearly laid down provisions for such accession to WTO. Now China will have to make further changes in its existing economic system—a command economy—albeit since 1978, it has been constantly pursuing the policy of liberalization. China, in fact, has two sets of economic systems working simultaneously. One is as free as the market economy of USA and second is totally state-owned economy. In the command economy segment, the output is produced as per the pre-decided targets, not taking into consideration the market demand and quality. In this segment of the economy, there is always a likelihood of overproduction or underproduction. China has always overproduced for avoiding any shortage. It, in turn, results in the filling of the inventories. This overproduction is the main root of the menace of hostile dumping by China being experienced by India in particular and the world in general. This hostile dumping would come under sharp scrutiny after China join WTO.

The sate-owned part of the economy does not reflect the true price of produce. Now that China has joined WTO, it will have to show the real price of its produce and pursue the world standards for accounting practices. It is believed that in China the infantry works in factories in peace time. Though they get only one salary, they are simultaneously performing two jobs. The labour cost, thus, does not make part of the total cost, thereby reducing the price per unit of produce. Moreover, in China, equity culture is at nascent stage. The capital is arranged mainly through the bank loans. The commercial banks in China are accounting for one of the highest NPAs in the world. The enterprises are inclined not to repay bank loans and thus save the cost of interest and principal itself. These practices will have to be done away with forthwith.

China keeps its exchange rate over-valued. Even in the wake of the South-East Asian Crisis, when all its major partners did the downward revision of their currencies, it did not devalue its Yuan. Though, at that time, it helped the world economy and saved it from further slipping into the recession, it seems to be an undeclared strategy of China to remain competitive. The over-valuation of Yuan ensures the cheap imports of raw material and capital goods, whereas the impact on price of the exports are neutralized through keeping the price of produce at the artificially low level. This strategy in China is more effective because its imports are price inelastic, whereas its exports are price elastic. Now as China has joined the WTO and is required to do away with many practices non-compliant to the market economy and hiding the true price of the produce, it will have to discard this strategy. It will have to align its nominal exchange rate with its trading rivals' rates to remain competitive in the international market.

Among other implications of China joining WTO is the increased market access in China. China is the market of over one-and-a-half billion people. The purchasing power of China has been on the increase ever since the reform programmes were initiated in 1978. After joining WTO, China is bound to certain commitments including the market access through reducing and dismantling the tariff and non-tariff barriers. China has already reduced the tariffs substantially in its pursuit of entry in WTO. The average tariff level in China for industrial products was 16.6 per cent in 1998, which is planned to be further reduced to 9.5 per cent by 2005.[4] China is aligning its tariff level with that of East and South East Asian countries. It is also required to convert non-tariff barriers into the tariff equivalent. It would definitely give the element of certainty to the world business community as far as trading with China is concerned.

One of the most important areas getting affected as a result of China joining WTO is its intellectual property rights regime. Though China has shifted to the world standards as far as the laws relating to protection of the intellectual property rights are concerned in 1990s as a result of the bilateral agreement between US and China, the enforcement of laws is very poor. It is in spite of the fact that many intellectual property rights courts have been set up since 1993 in many provinces. After the US-China bilateral agreement in 1979, China enacted its Patent laws and trademark laws and joined the Paris Convention for the protection of intellectual protection in mid 1980s. It also adopted the international standards of copyrights by joining the Berne Copyright Convention and the Geneva Phonograms convention.[5] Now China having joined WTO, is obliged to give effective protection to intellectual right holders, which includes both legislative changes as well as proper enforcement of laws. In the bilateral agreement with the US on intellectual rights protection, China is committed to: Setting up new regime of enforcement for protection of intellectual property rights; Strengthening the effective control in border areas with the technical assistance from the US; permitting US audio-Video and software firms to enter Chinese market; eliminating import license for US audio and video products; imposing criminal penalties on copyright violators.

The accession document is about a thousand pages long containing China's obligations and commitments. The list of obligations is very long encompassing almost all sectors of the economy. However, it does not have enough time to meet them all. In of the majority cases, the deadline is 2005/2006 (in some cases, the obligations were to be carried-out immediately after accession). Within this time frame, the average tariffs in China have to come down to 9.5 per cent for the industrial goods and 17.5 per cent for the agriculture commodities, with peak tariff provision of 25 per cent only for cigarettes and automobiles. The services sector would be thrown wide open to foreign companies. For all practical purposes, the Chinese government has even foregone the right to intervene in investment decisions and the choice has been entirely left to the foreign investors. These obligations go beyond the existing obligations under various agreements for the other member countries. Some of the commitments taken by China are such that other WTO members (including the EU and the US) will take many years to meet them out. Take, for instance, its commitments in agriculture. Besides bringing down the average tariff to 17.5 per cent, China is also committed to open up trade including import, storage and distribution in most agriculture commodities to Chinese as well as foreign entities by 2005. Similarly, with respect to services, China has undertaken a broad range of commitments to remove practically all sorts of restrictions on such vital sectors as telecommunication, banking and insurance, retail and wholesale trading, and professional services, such as accountancy, legal counseling, audio-visual services, etc.[6] China has also agreed to apply WTO rules to state-owned enterprises and state-invested enterprises. It simply means that these enterprises will be required to function on the pure commercial bases, which is itself a serious challenge for China.

China's entry in WTO is going to create an imbalance of obligations among the member countries.[7] China's obligations may now, in many cases, set the standards for the commitments to be undertaken by other members in future negotiations. Logically, one of the immediate tasks of China as a WTO member should be to press for aggressive liberalization under WTO in view of the huge down-payment it has made for its entry in WTO. Only this strategy can restore the balance of obligations especially in areas of agriculture and services. It is estimated that China's current obligations can mean an increase in imports to the tune of $ 600 billion by 2005 from a current level of around $ 250 billion, and then it will continue to increase at its normal rate. For the rest of the world, especially the EU and the USA, it means a huge market access opportunity.

As far as China's market access in other member countries' markets after its entry in WTO is concerned, China is likely to lose its many competitive advantages due to the obligations to doing away with prohibited subsidies. Moreover, several transparency requirements would make it compulsory for China to show the true price of its commodities. Meeting out WTO obligations would mean adopting a full-fledged market economy for China by 2005. It would require a lot of legislative changes. It would not be a problem for China, given its political system. However, such a radical change in the economic system is fraught with risks in terms of social, economic and political destabilization, though a section of the economy is familiar with precepts of the market economy. Total economic liberalization without matching social and political transition can be a serious political challenge. The real issue facing China is whether it would be able to sustain a market economy under the present political system—a socialist one. Nowhere in the world is there an example for such an arrangement. It seems rather a paradox. Whether China will change its political system too to make it more consistent with the market economy is yet debatable. As far as the social implications are concerned, the major chunk of the population would taste the market economy first time. The market economy is a mixed bag having reward for innovative and pro-active individuals and punishments for laggards. In China, the mindset of the major part of its populace is still deep-rooted in socialist system with all its major economic features. Though the institutions can be changed through the legislative amendments in a short time, changing mindset takes generations. In the short and medium terms, till the people adequately adjust to the institutional changes in the economy, there would be unrest and destabilization in the society. There would be more losers than winners as a consequence of the altered situation in the short and medium terms.

Impact on South Asia

The entry of China in WTO would give an element of certainty to every member country, including the South Asian ones, in terms of market access and other aspects of the agreements. China is required to bind its tariff rates at the lower level. Some of the non-tariff barriers, which are not consistent with WTO, will have to be dismantled. It would certainly give more market access to the South Asian Countries in Chinese market. However, the real penetration in China's market would depend upon the efficiency and productivity of the South Asian enterprises, as the market access would be equal to all member countries of WTO. The potential items of exports for South Asia include processed agro-products, aquatic products,, cotton, raw cotton, pharmaceuticals and drugs, computer software, auto components, etc. China would also avail the same market access in South Asian Countries. After the removal of quantitative restrictions (QRs) in India, there is a fear that China's cheaper textile and other consumer goods would inundate the Indian market. India is already feeling the pinch of hostile dumping by China. Among the anti-dumping cases initiated by India, China accounts for the maximum cases. China has already carved out a large slice in the major foreign markets, particularly in the US and the EU. Once the Multi-Fibre Agreement is dismantled in 2005, the Chinese competition will be intensive in textile products in these markets.[8]

There is a feeling in the developing country that the entry of China in WTO would add a major weight in their collective bargaining power in the negotiations. This argument is fraught with skepticisms. The reason is now-a-days the traditional North-South divide does not work in the negotiations. It has been amply proved in the last Uruguay round negotiations and subsequent Ministerial Meets. Every country is guided by its own interests, and in pursuit of those interests, it can align with any country irrespective of whether it is developed or developing one. China is likely to behave in the same manner. Moreover, its interests are more close to the developed countries than the developing ones. It is also pursuing aggressively the policy of opening up its economy for trade and investment and would prefer to do the same under WTO, so that it could also get the equivalent access in member countries' markets.

NOTES AND REFERENCES

1. China's Entry in WTO: Implications for South AsiaMajie Zhu, East Asia Crisis and China, *The Post Cold War World*, (SIIS Publication, Shanghai, 2000, p.163.
2. Ibid., pp.170-75.
3. Ibid., p.172.
4. Bhaumik, T.K., New China on the Horizon, *The Economic Times*, Dec. 15, 2001.
5. Rui Pani, Sino-US Economic and Trade Relations: Basis for Bilateral Relations, *The Post Cold War World*, SIIS Publication, Shanghai, 2000, pp. 216-217.
6. Bhaumik, T.K., New China on the Horizon, *The Economic Times*, Dec. 15, 2001.
7. *Ibid.*
8. *South Asia Development and Cooperation Report 2001/02: RIS for Non-Aligned and Developed Countries*, New Delhi, p. 11.

Five

Cancun Fiasco

Implications for WTO and South Asia

After Seattle fiasco in Nov. 1999, it was the second jolt to the multilateral trading system, WTO, in Cancun, Mexico, within eight years of its coming into force. This time, the blow was so intense that it appeared the WTO, a nascent institution in its new incarnation, would not be able to recover from it, at least in the near future. However, the recently held Geneva talks, where the developed countries have accepted the demands of the developing countries in general in regard to the farm sector and agreed to drop the controversial issues of investment policy, competition policy and transparency in government procurement from the final agenda for negotiations, have again given a breath of life to it.[1]

The Seattle failure was undone to some extent by the Doha Meet in 2001, which could launch a new round on limited issues.[2] The Cancun Meet was the sequel of Doha Meet, where the issues unresolved in the Doha Meet were to be settled, and on many issues, on which the members showed their acceptance, the final negotiations were to take place. However, it was unfortunate that the differences between the developed and developing countries could not be bridged, and an impasse again emerged. It did not seem an easy task this time to break the stalemate, as all issues involved were the sensitive ones. Some of the observers feared lest the plateau had reached in the multilateral trading system. They were also of the opinion that the WTO would not be an effective forum for trade negotiations any more. It appeared that GATT was much more focused and acceptable institution than its successor, WTO, for its being a tightrope-walking for its members owing to its non-reversible nature of commitments and wider spectrum of coverage. It seemed that the deadline (31st Dec., 2004) for completing the Doha round would not be met, albeit the Uruguay round also took longer time than the original time frame earmarked for it.

For this deadlock, the developed countries should share more blame than their developing counterparts. It is because most of the promises made bv them ever since the WTO came into being were not translated into reality. While they were not meeting their earlier commitments, they were keen to usher the members into new areas, apparently inimical to the developing countries' interests.

As per the World Bank report, 'a successful completion of the Doha Round of negotiations could raise the global income by more than $ 500 billion a year by 2015. Out of this, over 60 per cent would go to the poor countries, helping to pull 144 million people out of poverty. These benefits to the poor countries were supposed to accrue from the reduction of rich countries' farm subsidies, more open markets in the North and freer trade among poor countries.[3] The estimates of the World Bank might be true on paper. However, in reality, the first two routes, through which the gains were predicted to be realized, were not opened by the rich countries to the extent of their commitments. On the contrary, in some areas, the barriers were rather raised. For example, the subsidies in agriculture sector in America and the EU have gone up over the last many years. Moreover, though the average tariffs have come down in these countries, high tariffs, tariff peaks, tariff escalation and non-tariff barriers are practically denying the market access to the commodities originating from the developing countries, including South Asian countries. Still more, the anti-dumping and countervailing provisions are being used by the rich countries injudiciously so often against the commodities coming from the developing countries that they inflict the irreparable damage to their interests. In this scenario, the tall claims made by the north-controlled multilateral agencies in a bid to woo the poor countries look an eyewash.

In fact, the poor countries, including South Asian ones, are not against the multilateral trading system. They are well aware of the fact that WTO is a more fair and democratic system than the earlier GATT and conducts negotiations bilaterally. In the GATT system, the developed countries would make decisions themselves with little consultations with poor countries. In the bilateral negotiations, the relative economic clouts of the parties play an important role. In this situation, there is every possibility that the terms and conditions would always be tilted in favour of the developed countries. Thus, WTO is a more favoured system among the poor countries. However, they want the developed countries to fulfill their promises first in various areas, and then go into new agreements. By any logic, it seems to be justified also.

The Reasons for Fiasco

Though the speed of failure of the Meet caught even the seasoned trade negotiators by surprise, seeds of disagreements were sown long before start of the Cancun Meet. The launch of the Doha round was itself a nail-biting negotiation.

The agenda involved was very grand: Doha would reduce trade-distorting farm support, slash tariffs on farm goods and eliminate export subsidies; it would cut industrial tariffs, especially in areas relevant to poor countries, such as textiles; it would free trade in services, and it would negotiate global rules (subject to a framework to be decided through consensus among members) on Singapore issues—competition policy, investment policy, transparency in government procurement and trade facilitation.

From the start, the members were not ready to accept the major part of the Doha agenda. The EU, for example, denied that it had ever promised to eliminate export subsidies.[4] The poor countries, along with South Asian countries, refused that they ever agreed to talk on Singapore issues. Rather they were more interested on the implementation of issues of earlier agreements. Japan was hell-bent to say no to any cuts in rice tariffs. Thus, these uncompromising stances by diverse interest groups from the beginning left heavy burden on the Cancun meeting. In four-days time, over which the Meet was spanned, only a miracle could achieve what could not be materialized in 22-months after Doha Meet.[5] The deadlock was inevitable.

The issue of agriculture subsidies was the most sensitive before and during the Cancun Meet. After months of impasse, at the intensive persuasion from the poor countries, the US and the EU drew up a framework in August 2003 for freeing agriculture trade. The plan included much less than what was promised in the Doha Declaration. For instance, it did not talk about dismantling of the export subsidies at all. A new group—G-21, led by India, China and Brazil, denounced the plan as backtracking to their Doha promises. The G-21 group emerged as a powerful voice in the Meet as it represented half of the world' population and two-thirds of its farmers. Though the countries of the G-21 were having diverse interests, they strongly demanded that rich countries cut their farm subsidies in a substantial manner.

This time, one more group comprising the African countries emerged as a strong voice for agriculture, albeit its reasons were different. They were worried that freeing farm trade would mean losing their special preferences in the developed countries' markets. The developed countries accord special preferences to many African countries. For example, EU's former colonies get special access to the EU's markets for their bananas. They also had fear that cutting tariffs would ruin their small farm economies. Many of them, especially the Western African countries, were concerned about their cotton. After much efforts, they could get cotton included in the Cancun agenda for discussion. The US doles out over $ 3 billion worth subsidies a year to its cotton farmers, which keep the world price of cotton depressed. The W. African countries wanted the US to speedily dismantle this subsidy and pay compensation for the damage it had caused so far. However, contrary to their expectations, the draft text came as a big disappointment for them, as it only promised a WTO review on the textile sector. It also suggested that W. African countries should diversify into other crops also.

Angered at the stance of rich countries on cotton, the African countries declined to lend their support on the new Singapore issues. EU was most interested on these new issues, but it was not ready to compromise on other issues relevant to the poor countries. At the eleventh hour, to save the meeting from failure, EU agreed to jettison three most controversial issues—competition policy, investment policy and transparency in government procurement—out of the four. However, the indisputable issue of trade facilitation also could not be accepted for negotiation in the overall atmosphere of disagreement.

From Cancun to Where

Though the last date for the completion of the Doha round is 31st December 2004, given the uncompromising stances of various parties, the chances of meeting the deadline are very slim. The optimists can take solace from Uruguay Round negotiations, which also took longer time to complete than the planned time-frame. However, this time, the breaking of stalemate did not look an easy task, as the developing countries were feeling cheated because of the developed countries not fulfilling their earlier commitments, especially in the agriculture sector. The developed countries understood it and attempted to break the ice through acceding to major demands of the developing countries in general in farm sector in the recently held Geneva talks. The developed countries should realize that in the game of continuous negotiations, you can not expect other party to accept all your demands all the times, while you yourself keep on backtracking to your earlier commitments. It is not the essence of negotiation. One can not befool the other party all the time. Making the multilateral trading system an effective organization for trade negotiations is the responsibility of all members. In fact, morally, the responsibility lies more with the developed members because they are better off.

One of the inevitable outcome of the failure of Cancun Meet was the renewed impetus to the trade negotiations through regional trading blocs and bilateral negotiations. As has been analyzed earlier, it is not in the interest of the poor countries. They would be more marginalized in the world trade, especially in the developed countries' markets owing to the trade diversion towards the members of the trading blocs of rich countries. It is because of their meeting a major part of import needs within the bloc owing to more complementaries among these economies.[6] This would definitely put the developing countries at the receiving end, deteriorating their trade balance and Balance-of-Payment (BOP) positions. However, for the developed countries also, it would not give a lasting solution, because for having economic growth through international trade route (which is the prominent route left for them at their present level of economic development), a trading bloc can not give much scope. They will have to open up their economies at the world level, and for that purpose, they would have to give due attention to the interests of their developing and least-developed counterparts. It is what they have shown in the recent Geneva talks.

NOTES AND REFERENCES

1. 'Acceptable Agenda', *The Times of India,* August 4, 2004,p. 14.
2. *South Asia Development and Cooperation Report 2001/02: RIS for Non-Aligned and Developed Countries* (New Delhi), p. 17.
3. 'The World Trade Under Fire', *The Economist,* September 20, 2003, p. 29.
4. 'Cancun's Charming Outcome', *The Economist,* September 20, 2003, p. 13.
5. *Ibid.* p. 13.
6. Gupta, Anshuman, *SAARC: SAPTA to SAFTA,* Shipra Publications, New Delhi, 2002, p. 63.

Conclusion

The foregoing analysis clearly brings out the beneficial character of the opening up of trade at the multilateral level under WTO, as it promotes economic advancement at the world level and avoids the negative consequences arising out of the economic cooperation at the regional and bilateral levels. However, it is advisable for the developing countries, including South Asian ones, to ensure adequate safeguards to protect their interests. For serving their interests, it is necessary that they work collectively with properly chalking out their strategy on each issue after intensive research. The developing countries, especially the SAARC nations, showed coherence in their positions on each issue at the Seattle, Doha and Cancun Meets. As a result, they could win many concessions in the Doha Meet. The most contentious issue of labour standards was forced to be dropped from the final agenda for negotiations. Now it would be the concern of ILO. The Singapore issues including Competition Policy, Investment Policy, Trade Facilitation and Transparency in Government Procurement were shelved for another two years until the next Ministerial Conference to be held in 2003, where the modalities of the negotiations were to be decided with consensus among member countries. However, even at Cancun, no consensus could be reached over these issues resulting in failure of this Meet in 2003. With their concerted efforts, the developing countries were able to secure major benefits in reviewing the existing agreements.

It is desirable for the developing countries to try collectively for inclusion of extra provisions in WTO to mitigate the negative consequences of a regional trading blocs (RTBs) among the developed countries as a result of trade diversion. The two conditions for establishing a bloc under Article XXIV of WTO are not adequate to protect their interests. It would be proper to include more measures in it to ensure that developed countries do not misuse it against the developing ones through giving more concessions to member countries. The condition on the basis of average alone would not be effective in preventing the developed countries from manipulating the bloc in their favour. A mechanism should be devised to check the tendency on their part to shield their economies behind the tariff peaks and tariff escalation.

The South Asian countries should intensify the efforts to re-energize the regional trading grouping in the region—SAPTA—which has failed to deliver for a long time. In spite of its coming in force almost nine years back in 1995, it could not go a long way in terms of opening up economies within the region, though the original plan was to upgrade it into SAFTA—SAARC Free Trade Area—by 1999. Even the revised plan to convert it into SAFTA by 2004 is unlikely to be achieved. It is not even half way through in terms of opening up all trade within the region, a requisite for acquiring the status of SAFTA. In fact, a regional trading bloc gives an opportunity to its members to sharpen their competitiveness both at the price and quality fronts through specialization and economies of scale in the sectors they have comparative advantages in. It is of strategic importance for the developing countries to open up their economies first within the region. As all the economies within the region are likely to have more or less comparable level of economic advancement, there is less danger for relatively less developed economies of being swamped by foreign goods originating from the better off countries of the region. In fact, the South Asian countries should synchronize opening up their economies in such a way that liberalizing economies within the region should precede opening up under the WTO by quite a margin of time period, say 5 to

10 years. However, it is other way round in the case of the South Asian bloc. While under WTO, the tariffs on all agriculture goods and almost half of the industrial goods have been bound and the non-tariff barriers pledged to be dismantled, under SAPTA, not even fifty per cent of the tariff lines have been covered, not to speak of the non-tariff barriers, which are more prominent in the region. The region will be well-advised not to leave any stone unturned to make the regional economic integration process a success at a faster pace, sinking all their bilateral territorial discords.

Though the collapse of talks in Cancun again caused some uncertainty about the future of the WTO, the organization is going to exist as an effective forum for trade negotiations, as all parties soon realized its significance in the recently held Geneva talks. The developed countries seem to have realized their mistakes and more or less acceded all the demands of the developing countries especially in the farm sector. They also agreed to drop the sensitive Singapore issues, including investment policy, competition policy and transparency in government procurement, from the final agenda for negotiations. Although, the negotiations at the regional and bilateral levels got a renewed impetus in the wake of the Cancun fiasco, the imperatives for going back to multilateral forum could not be ignored for long. The developed countries at Geneva realized their major responsibility in making the WTO institution a success and tried to meet their earlier commitments in true spirit. There is, in fact, much justification for the developed countries not to be in a hurry in raising new issues. Sufficient time is needed for the poor countries to adjust their economies to their earlier commitments.

The South Asian countries are undergoing the process of liberalization and globalization in varying degrees. Though they are opening up their economies voluntarily, they feel apprehensive in giving any commitment under WTO owing to its non-reversible nature. It is worthwhile specially for the developing nations (India, Pakistan and Sri Lanka) of the region to expedite the process of opening up their economies voluntarily so as to narrow down the gap between the requirements of their economies and likely provisions of the agreements on issues of competition and investment policies. Thought these issues have been dropped for the time being, they are likely to crop up again in the future. It is advisable for the South Asian states to adopt a pro-active approach by continuing the search for like-minded states beyond the region, preparing well on each issue and responding collectively at future talks.

In fact, negotiations at present are becoming highly complicated and technical. To know the intricacies involved in each issue and taking the most appropriate stance on it require intensive research. As the poor countries can not conduct research on an individual basis for want of enough resources—financial as well as technical—they should collectively set up a fund for this specific purpose and involve the experts from all like-minded countries. The pooling of resources at the regional level on a regular basis would be a viable option for the South Asian countries. For this purpose, a close coordination among governments, industry, and academic and research bodies is crucial.

The region should strengthen its agriculture sector to fully reap the benefits under agreement on agriculture (AOA). The countries of the region should implement the reforms programme in the farm sector as well to do away with many ills plaguing it. Institutional support should be augmented in the areas of credit to the farmers, marketing, research and development, etc. A partnership between the corporate sector and farming would be the most viable option. Here also, a coordinated approach at the regional level would go a long way to exploit the benefits. Exporting agriculture commodities in bulk would not bring much economic gains. They can be processed, packaged and marketed with a brand name at the regional level. In this way, the traders can avoid the competition among themselves, which generally leads to lower prices of their products.

Likewise, there is need for a well coordinated integrated textile strategy at the national as well as regional levels to make the textile sector competitive in the post-MFA regime. The textile sector, the second most important sector after agriculture in terms of exchange earning for the South Asian countries, is in urgent need of modernization, technical restructuring and financial support. Facilities for training and retraining the labour for more skilled jobs need to be strengthened.

The new IPR regime, based both on the process and product patents, is going to come into full swing after 2005. It is an area the South Asian region is most scared of. The region needs to develop greater clarity in respect of identifying the long term interests of the region without losing sight of the short term ones. For this purpose, strengthening our institutional facility for patent registration, copyright protection and legal process of dispute settlement should be emphasized on an urgent basis. The relationship between industry and research and development activities should be fostered, as the days of government sponsored research are gone. The region should map its bio diversity resources adequately and an inventory on the profile of community knowledge should be set up. Emphasis should be laid on the bio technological research. The investment on the R&D activities as a proportion of GDP in South Asia is one of the lowest in the world. As future competition would be based on technology, there is an immediate requirement to step up the investment on R&D.

In the services sector, the most adversely affected area because of the General Agreement on Trade in Services (GATS) is the financial sector. The negotiators should tread cautiously in this sector. They should synchronize the reforms underway in the financial sector with commitments under GATS. For example, the domestic banking sector in the region is burdened with many social obligations. The entry of the foreign banks would be without any social obligations, which would definitely put the foreign banks at an advantageous position. Thus there is need to effect reforms in the banking sector of the region to provide it the level playing field.

Though the anti-dumping measures were included under WTO with a benign intention, they were misused by the developed countries as a new form of non-tariff barrier (NTB) especially to the commodities coming from the developing countries, including the South Asian ones.

It was one of the agenda issues under implementation in the Doha Meet. The issue is still un-resolved. There is an urgent need to streamline the situation as the frequent use of these provisions for the same commodity disrupts the supply of that commodity. This practice, more often than not, forces the firms concerned to close down (as they do not possess enough financial resources to sustain for a long time and are generally 100 per cent export-oriented). On the other side of the coin, the developing countries do not have the required financial resources as well as expertise to unravel the cases of anti-dumping and start investigation on them. The South Asian countries can set up an institution at the regional level to monitor the dumping cases and for identifying suitable anti-dumping measures to avoid the damage. The cost of fighting cases under WTO is very high. The South Asian countries not only lack required financial resources but also the legal expertise to fight cases at the WTO. It is high time that the South Asian universities introduce the WTO subjects in the curricula for their law and master degree programmes. Funds at the national and regional levels can also be created to help fight the anti-dumping cases.

Annexure I

World Trade Organization
Ministerial Conference

Doha, 9-14 November 2001

MINISTERIAL DECLARATION
Adopted on 14 November 2001

1. The multilateral trading system embodied in the World Trade Organization has contributed significantly to economic growth, development and employment throughout the past fifty years. We are determined, particularly in the light of the global economic slowdown, to maintain the process of reform and liberalization of trade policies, thus ensuring that the system plays its full part in promoting recovery, growth and development. We therefore strongly reaffirm the principles and objectives set out in the Marrakesh Agreement Establishing the World Trade Organization, and pledge to reject the use of protectionism.

2. International trade can play a major role in the promotion of economic development and the alleviation of poverty. We recognize the need for all our peoples to benefit from the increased opportunities and welfare gains that the multilateral trading system generates. The majority of WTO Members are developing countries. We seek to place their needs and interests at the heart of the Work Programme adopted in this Declaration. Recalling the Preamble to the Marrakesh

Agreement, we shall continue to make positive efforts designed to ensure that developing countries, and especially the least-developed among them, secure a share in the growth of world trade commensurate with the needs of their economic development. In this context, enhanced market access, balanced rules, and well targeted, sustainably financed technical assistance and capacity-building programmes have important roles to play.

3. We recognize the particular vulnerability of the least-developed countries and the special structural difficulties they face in the global economy. We are committed to addressing the marginalization of least-developed countries in international trade and to improving their effective participation in the multilateral trading system. We recall the commitments made by Ministers at our meetings in Marrakesh, Singapore and Geneva, and by the international community at the Third UN Conference on Least-Developed Countries in Brussels, to help least-developed countries secure beneficial and meaningful integration into the multilateral trading system and the global economy. We are determined that the WTO will play its part in building effectively on these commitments under the Work Programme we are establishing.

4. We stress our commitment to the WTO as the unique forum for global trade rule-making and liberalization, while also recognizing that regional trade agreements can play an important role in promoting the liberalization and expansion of trade and in fostering development.

5. We are aware that the challenges Members face in a rapidly changing international environment cannot be addressed through measures taken in the trade field alone. We shall continue to work with the Bretton Woods institutions for greater coherence in global economic policy-making.

6. We strongly reaffirm our commitment to the objective of sustainable development, as stated in the Preamble to the Marrakesh Agreement. We are convinced that the aims of upholding and safeguarding an open and non-discriminatory multilateral trading system, and acting for the protection of the environment and the promotion of sustainable development can and must be mutually

supportive. We take note of the efforts by Members to conduct national environmental assessments of trade policies on a voluntary basis. We recognize that under WTO rules no country should be prevented from taking measures for the protection of human, animal or plant life or health, or of the environment at the levels it considers appropriate, subject to the requirement that they are not applied in a manner which would constitute a means of arbitrary or unjustifiable discrimination between countries where the same conditions prevail, or a disguised restriction on international trade, and are otherwise in accordance with the provisions of the WTO Agreements. We welcome the WTO's continued cooperation with UNEP and other inter-governmental environmental organizations. We encourage efforts to promote cooperation between the WTO and relevant international environmental and developmental organizations, especially in the lead-up to the World Summit on Sustainable Development to be held in Johannesburg, South Africa, in September 2002.

7. We reaffirm the right of Members under the General Agreement on Trade in Services to regulate, and to introduce new regulations on, the supply of services.

8. We reaffirm our declaration made at the Singapore Ministerial Conference regarding internationally recognized core labour standards. We take note of work under way in the International Labour Organization (ILO) on the social dimension of globalization.

9. We note with particular satisfaction that this Conference has completed the WTO accession procedures for China and Chinese Taipei. We also welcome the accession as new Members, since our last Session, of Albania, Croatia, Georgia, Jordan, Lithuania, Moldova and Oman, and note the extensive market-access commitments already made by these countries on accession. These accessions will greatly strengthen the multilateral trading system, as will those of the 28 countries now negotiating their accession. We therefore attach great importance to concluding accession proceedings as quickly as possible. In particular, we are committed to accelerating the accession of least-developed countries.

10. Recognizing the challenges posed by an expanding WTO membership, we confirm our collective responsibility to ensure internal transparency and the effective participation of all Members. While emphasizing the intergovernmental character of the organization, we are committed to making the WTO's operations more transparent, including through more effective and prompt dissemination of information, and to improve dialogue with the public. We shall therefore at the national and multilateral levels continue to promote á better public understanding of the WTO and to communicate the benefits of a liberal, rules-based multilateral trading system.

11. In view of these considerations, we hereby agree to undertake the broad and balanced Work Programme set out below. This incorporates both an expanded negotiating agenda and other important decisions and activities necessary to address the challenges facing the multilateral trading system.

Work Programme

Implementation-Related Issues and Concerns

12. We attach the utmost importance to the implementation-related issues and concerns raised by Members and are determined to find appropriate solutions to them.. In this connection, and having regard to the General Council Decisions of 3 May and 15 December 2000, we further adopt the Decision on Implementation-Related Issues and Concerns in document WT/MIN(01)/17 to address a number of implementation problems faced by Members. We agree that negotiations on outstanding implementation issues shall be an integral part of the Work Programme we are establishing, and that agreements reached at an early stage in these negotiations shall be treated in accordance with the provisions of paragraph 47 below. In this regard, we shall proceed as follows: (a) where we provide a specific negotiating mandate in this Declaration, the relevant implementation issues shall be addressed under that mandate; (b) the other outstanding implementation issues shall be

addressed as a matter of priority by the relevant WTO bodies, which shall report to the Trade Negotiations Committee, established under paragraph 46 below, by the end of 2002 for appropriate action.

Agriculture

13. We recognize the work already undertaken in the negotiations initiated in early 2000 under Article 20 of the Agreement on Agriculture, including the large number of negotiating proposals submitted on behalf of a total of 121 Members. We recall the long-term objective referred to in the Agreement to establish a fair and market-oriented trading system through a programme of fundamental reform encompassing strengthened rules and specific commitments on support and protection in order to correct and prevent restrictions and distortions in world agricultural markets. We reconfirm our commitment to this programme. Building on the work carried out to date and without prejudging the outcome of the negotiations we commit ourselves to comprehensive negotiations aimed at: substantial improvements in market access; reductions of, with a view to phasing out, all forms of export subsidies; and substantial reductions in trade-distorting domestic support. We agree that special and differential treatment for developing countries shall be an integral part of all elements of the negotiations and shall be embodied in the Schedules of concessions and commitments and as appropriate in the rules and disciplines to be negotiated, so as to be operationally effective and to enable developing countries to effectively take account of their development needs, including food security and rural development. We take note of the non-trade concerns reflected in the negotiating proposals submitted by Members and confirm that non-trade concerns will be taken into account in the negotiations as provided for in the Agreement on Agriculture.

14. Modalities for the further commitments, including provisions for special and differential treatment, shall be established no later than 31 March 2003. Participants shall submit their comprehensive draft Schedules based on these modalities no later than the date of the Fifth

Session of the Ministerial Conference. The negotiations, including with respect to rules and disciplines and related legal texts, shall be concluded as part and at the date of conclusion of the negotiating agenda as a whole.

Services

15. The negotiations on trade in services shall be conducted with a view to promoting the economic growth of all trading partners and the development of developing and least-developed countries. We recognize the work already undertaken in the negotiations, initiated in January 2000 under Article XIX of the General Agreement on Trade in Services, and the large number of proposals submitted by Members on a wide range of sectors and several horizontal issues, as well as on movement of natural persons. We reaffirm the Guidelines and Procedures for the Negotiations adopted by the Council for Trade in Services on 28 March 2001 as the basis for continuing the negotiations, with a view to achieving the objectives of the General Agreement on Trade in Services, as stipulated in the Preamble, Article IV and Article XIX of that Agreement. Participants shall submit initial requests for specific commitments by 30 June 2002 and initial offers by 31 March 2003.

Market Access for Non-agricultural Products

16. We agree to negotiations which shall aim, by modalities to be agreed, to reduce or as appropriate eliminate tariffs, including the reduction or elimination of tariff peaks, high tariffs, and tariff escalation, as well as non-tariff barriers, in particular on products of export interest to developing countries. Product coverage shall be comprehensive and without *a priori* exclusions. The negotiations shall take fully into account the special needs and interests of developing and least-developed country participants, including through less than full reciprocity in reduction commitments, in accordance with the relevant provisions of Article XXVIII *bis* of GATT 1994 and the provisions

cited in paragraph 50 below. To this end, the modalities to be agreed will include appropriate studies and capacity-building measures to assist least-developed countries to participate effectively in the negotiations.

Trade-Related Aspects of Intellectual Property Rights

17. We stress the importance we attach to implementation and interpretation of the Agreement on Trade-Related Aspects of Intellectual Property Rights (TRIPS Agreement) in a manner supportive of public health, by promoting both access to existing medicines and research and development into new medicines and, in this connection, are adopting a separate Declaration.

18. With a view to completing the work started in the Council for Trade-Related Aspects of Intellectual Property Rights (Council for TRIPS) on the implementation of Article 23.4, we agree to negotiate the establishment of a multilateral system of notification and registration of geographical indications for wines and spirits by the Fifth Session of the Ministerial Conference. We note that issues related to the extension of the protection of geographical indications provided for in Article 23 to products other than wines and spirits will be addressed in the Council for TRIPS pursuant to paragraph 12 of this Declaration.

19. We instruct the Council for TRIPS, in pursuing its work programme including under the review of Article 27.3(b), the review of the implementation of the TRIPS Agreement under Article 71.1 and the work foreseen pursuant to paragraph 12 of this Declaration, to examine, *inter alia*, the relationship between the TRIPS Agreement and the Convention on Biological Diversity, the protection of traditional knowledge and folklore, and other relevant new developments raised by Members pursuant to Article 71.1. In undertaking this work, the TRIPS Council shall be guided by the objectives and principles set out in Articles 7 and 8 of the TRIPS Agreement and shall take fully into account the development dimension.

Relationship between Trade and Investment

20. Recognizing the case for a multilateral framework to secure transparent, stable and predictable conditions for long-term cross-border investment, particularly foreign direct investment, that will contribute to the expansion of trade, and the need for enhanced technical assistance and capacity-building in this area as referred to in paragraph 21, we agree that negotiations will take place after the Fifth Session of the Ministerial Conference on the basis of a decision to be taken, by explicit consensus, at that Session on modalities of negotiations.

21. We recognize the needs of developing and least-developed countries for enhanced support for technical assistance and capacity building in this area, including policy analysis and development so that they may better evaluate the implications of closer multilateral cooperation for their development policies and objectives, and human and institutional development. To this end, we shall work in cooperation with other relevant intergovernmental organisations, including UNCTAD, and through appropriate regional and bilateral channels, to provide strengthened and adequately resourced assistance to respond to these needs.

22. In the period until the Fifth Session, further work in the Working Group on the Relationship Between Trade and Investment will focus on the clarification of: scope and definition; transparency; non-discrimination; modalities for pre-establishment commitments based on a GATS-type, positive list approach; development provisions; exceptions and balance-of-payments safeguards; consultation and the settlement of disputes between Members. Any framework should reflect in a balanced manner the interests of home and host countries, and take due account of the development policies and objectives of host governments as well as their right to regulate in the public interest. The special development, trade and financial needs of developing and least-developed countries should be taken into account as an integral part of any framework, which should enable Members to undertake obligations and commitments commensurate with their individual needs

and circumstances. Due regard should be paid to other relevant WTO provisions. Account should be taken, as appropriate, of existing bilateral and regional arrangements on investment.

Interaction between Trade and Competition Policy

23. Recognizing the case for a multilateral framework to enhance the contribution of competition policy to international trade and development, and the need for enhanced technical assistance and capacity-building in this area as referred to in paragraph 24, we agree that negotiations will take place after the Fifth Session of the Ministerial Conference on the basis of a decision to be taken, by explicit consensus, at that Session on modalities of negotiations.

24. We recognize the needs of developing and least-developed countries for enhanced support for technical assistance and capacity building in this area, including policy analysis and development so that they may better evaluate the implications of closer multilateral cooperation for their development policies and objectives, and human and institutional development. To this end, we shall work in cooperation with other relevant intergovernmental organisations, including UNCTAD, and through appropriate regional and bilateral channels, to provide strengthened and adequately resourced assistance to respond to these needs.

25. In the period until the Fifth Session, further work in the Working Group on the Interaction between Trade and Competition Policy will focus on the clarification of: core principles, including transparency, non-discrimination and procedural fairness, and provisions on hardcore cartels; modalities for voluntary cooperation; and support for progressive reinforcement of competition institutions in developing countries through capacity building. Full account shall be taken of the needs of developing and least-developed country participants and appropriate flexibility provided to address them.

Transparency in Government Procurement

26. Recognizing the case for a multilateral agreement on transparency in government procurement and the need for enhanced technical assistance and capacity building in this area, we agree that negotiations will take place after the Fifth Session of the Ministerial Conference on the basis of a decision to be taken, by explicit consensus, at that Session on modalities of negotiations. These negotiations will build on the progress made in the Working Group on Transparency in Government Procurement by that time and take into account participants' development priorities, especially those of least-developed country participants. Negotiations shall be limited to the transparency aspects and therefore will not restrict the scope for countries to give preferences to domestic supplies and suppliers. We commit ourselves to ensuring adequate technical assistance and support for capacity building both during the negotiations and after their conclusion.

Trade Facilitation

27. Recognizing the case for further expediting the movement, release and clearance of goods, including goods in transit, and the need for enhanced technical assistance and capacity building in this area, we agree that negotiations will take place after the Fifth Session of the Ministerial Conference on the basis of a decision to be taken, by explicit consensus, at that Session on modalities of negotiations. In the period until the Fifth Session, the Council for Trade in Goods shall review and as appropriate, clarify and improve relevant aspects of Articles V, VIII and X of the GATT 1994 and identify the trade facilitation needs and priorities of Members, in particular developing and least-developed countries. We commit ourselves to ensuring adequate technical assistance and support for capacity building in this area.

WTO Rules

28. In the light of experience and of the increasing application of these instruments by Members, we agree to negotiations aimed at clarifying and improving disciplines under the Agreements on Implementation of Article VI of the GATT 1994 and on Subsidies and Countervailing Measures, while preserving the basic concepts, principles and effectiveness of these Agreements and their instruments and objectives, and taking into account the needs of developing and least-developed participants. In the initial phase of the negotiations, participants will indicate the provisions, including disciplines on trade distorting practices, that they seek to clarify and improve in the subsequent phase. In the context of these negotiations, participants shall also aim to clarify and improve WTO disciplines on fisheries subsidies, taking into account the importance of this sector to developing countries. We note that fisheries subsidies are also referred to in paragraph 31.

29. We also agree to negotiations aimed at clarifying and improving disciplines and procedures under the existing WTO provisions applying to regional trade agreements. The negotiations shall take into account the developmental aspects of regional trade agreements.

Dispute Settlement Understanding

30. We agree to negotiations on improvements and clarifications of the Dispute Settlement Understanding. The negotiations should be based on the work done thus far as well as any additional proposals by Members, and aim to agree on improvements and clarifications not later than May 2003, at which time we will take steps to ensure that the results enter into force as soon as possible thereafter.

Trade and Environment

31. With a view to enhancing the mutual supportiveness of trade and environment, we agree to negotiations, without prejudging their outcome, on:

(i) the relationship between existing WTO rules and specific trade obligations set out in multilateral environmental agreements (MEAs). The negotiations shall be limited in scope to the applicability of such existing WTO rules as among parties to the MEA in question. The negotiations shall not prejudice the WTO rights of any Member that is not a party to the MEA in question;

(ii) procedures for regular information exchange between MEA Secretariats and the relevant WTO committees, and the criteria for the granting of observer status;

(iii) the reduction or, as appropriate, elimination of tariff and non-tariff barriers to environmental goods and services.

We note that fisheries subsidies form part of the negotiations provided for in paragraph 28.

32. We instruct the Committee on Trade and Environment, in pursuing work on all items on its agenda within its current terms of reference, to give particular attention to:

(i) the effect of environmental measures on market access, especially in relation to developing countries, in particular the least-developed among them, and those situations in which the elimination or reduction of trade restrictions and distortions would benefit trade, the environment and development;

(ii) the relevant provisions of the Agreement on Trade-Related Aspects of Intellectual Property Rights; and

(iii) labelling requirements for environmental purposes.

Work on these issues should include the identification of any need to clarify relevant WTO rules. The Committee shall report to the Fifth Session of the Ministerial Conference, and make recommendations, where appropriate, with respect to future action, including the desirability of negotiations. The outcome of this work as well as the negotiations carried out under paragraph 31(i) and (ii) shall be compatible with the open and non-discriminatory nature of the multilateral trading system, shall not add to or diminish the rights and obligations of Members under existing WTO agreements, in particular the Agreement on the Application of Sanitary and Phytosanitary Measures, nor alter the balance of these rights and obligations, and will take into account the needs of developing and least-developed countries.

33. We recognize the importance of technical assistance and capacity building in the field of trade and environment to developing countries, in particular the least-developed among them. We also encourage that expertise and experience be shared with Members wishing to perform environmental reviews at the national level. A report shall be prepared on these activities for the Fifth Session.

Electronic Commerce

34. We take note of the work which has been done in the General Council and other relevant bodies since the Ministerial Declaration of 20 May 1998 and agree to continue the Work Programme on Electronic Commerce. The work to date demonstrates that electronic commerce creates new challenges and opportunities for trade for Members at all stages of development, and we recognize the importance of creating and maintaining an environment which is favourable to the future development of electronic commerce. We instruct the General Council to consider the most appropriate institutional arrangements for handling the Work Programme, and to report on further progress to the Fifth Session of the Ministerial Conference. We declare that Members will

maintain their current practice of not imposing customs duties on electronic transmissions until the Fifth Session.

Small Economies

35. We agree to a work programme, under the auspices of the General Council, to examine issues relating to the trade of small economies. The objective of this work is to frame responses to the trade-related issues identified for the fuller integration of small, vulnerable economies into the multilateral trading system, and not to create a sub-category of WTO Members. The General Council shall review the work programme and make recommendations for action to the Fifth Session of the Ministerial Conference.

Trade, Debt and Finance

36. We agree to an examination, in a Working Group under the auspices of the General Council, of the relationship between trade, debt and finance, and of any possible recommendations on steps that might be taken within the mandate and competence of the WTO to enhance the capacity of the multilateral trading system to contribute to a durable solution to the problem of external indebtedness of developing and least-developed countries, and to strengthen the coherence of international trade and financial policies, with a view to safeguarding the multilateral trading system from the effects of financial and monetary instability. The General Council shall report to the Fifth Session of the Ministerial Conference on progress in the examination.

Trade and Transfer of Technology

37. We agree to an examination, in a Working Group under the auspices of the General Council, of the relationship between trade and transfer of technology, and of any possible recommendations on steps that might be taken within the mandate of the WTO to increase flows

of technology to developing countries. The General Council shall report to the Fifth Session of the Ministerial Conference on progress in the examination.

Technical Cooperation and Capacity Building

38. We confirm that technical cooperation and capacity building are core elements of the development dimension of the multilateral trading system, and we welcome and endorse the New Strategy for WTO Technical Cooperation for Capacity Building, Growth and Integration. We instruct the Secretariat, in coordination with other relevant agencies, to support domestic efforts for mainstreaming trade into national plans for economic development and strategies for poverty reduction. The delivery of WTO technical assistance shall be designed to assist developing and least-developed countries and low-income countries in transition to adjust to WTO rules and disciplines, implement obligations and exercise the rights of membership, including drawing on the benefits of an open, rules-based multilateral trading system. Priority shall also be accorded to small, vulnerable, and transition economies, as well as to Members and Observers without representation in Geneva. We reaffirm our support for the valuable work of the International Trade Centre, which should be enhanced.

39. We underscore the urgent necessity for the effective coordinated delivery of technical assistance with bilateral donors, in the OECD Development Assistance Committee and relevant international and regional intergovernmental institutions, within a coherent policy framework and timetable. In the coordinated delivery of technical assistance, we instruct the Director-General to consult with the relevant agencies, bilateral donors and beneficiaries, to identify ways of enhancing and rationalizing the Integrated Framework for Trade-Related Technical Assistance to Least-Developed Countries and the Joint Integrated Technical Assistance Programme (JITAP).

40. We agree that there is a need for technical assistance to benefit from secure and predictable funding. We therefore instruct the Committee

on Budget, Finance and Administration to develop a plan for adoption by the General Council in December 2001 that will ensure long-term funding for WTO technical assistance at an overall level no lower than that of the current year and commensurate with the activities outlined above.

41. We have established firm commitments on technical cooperation and capacity building in various paragraphs in this Ministerial Declaration. We reaffirm these specific commitments contained in paragraphs 16, 21, 24, 26, 27, 33, 38-40, 42 and 43, and also reaffirm the understanding in paragraph 2 on the important role of sustainably financed technical assistance and capacity-building programmes. We instruct the Director-General to report to the Fifth Session of the Ministerial Conference, with an interim report to the General Council in December 2002 on the implementation and adequacy of these commitments in the identified paragraphs.

Least-Developed Countries

42. We acknowledge the seriousness of the concerns expressed by the least-developed countries (LDCs) in the Zanzibar Declaration adopted by their Ministers in July 2001. We recognize that the integration of the LDCs into the multilateral trading system requires meaningful market access, support for the diversification of their production and export base, and trade-related technical assistance and capacity building. We agree that the meaningful integration of LDCs into the trading system and the global economy will involve efforts by all WTO Members. We commit ourselves to the objective of duty-free, quota-free market access for products originating from LDCs. In this regard, we welcome the significant market access improvements by WTO Members in advance of the Third UN Conference on LDCs (LDC-III), in Brussels, May 2001. We further commit ourselves to consider additional measures for progressive improvements in market access for LDCs. Accession of LDCs remains a priority for the Membership. We agree to work to facilitate and accelerate negotiations with acceding LDCs. We instruct the Secretariat to reflect the priority

we attach to LDCs' accessions in the annual plans for technical assistance. We reaffirm the commitments we undertook at LDC-III, and agree that the WTO should take into account, in designing its work programme for LDCs, the trade-related elements of the Brussels Declaration and Programme of Action, consistent with the WTO's mandate, adopted at LDC-III. We instruct the Sub-Committee for Least-Developed Countries to design such a work programme and to report on the agreed work programme to the General Council at its first meeting in 2002.

43. We endorse the Integrated Framework for Trade-Related Technical Assistance to Least-Developed Countries (IF) as a viable model for LDCs' trade development. We urge development partners to significantly increase contributions to the IF Trust Fund and WTO extra-budgetary trust funds in favour of LDCs. We urge the core agencies, in coordination with development partners, to explore the enhancement of the IF with a view to addressing the supply-side constraints of LDCs and the extension of the model to all LDCs, following the review of the IF and the appraisal of the ongoing Pilot Scheme in selected LDCs. We request the Director-General, following coordination with heads of the other agencies, to provide an interim report to the General Council in December 2002 and a full report to the Fifth Session of the Ministerial Conference on all issues affecting LDCs.

Special and Differential Treatment

44. We reaffirm that provisions for special and differential treatment are an integral part of the WTO Agreements. We note the concerns expressed regarding their operation in addressing specific constraints faced by developing countries, particularly least-developed countries. In that connection, we also note that some Members have proposed a Framework Agreement on Special and Differential Treatment (WT/GC/W/442). We therefore agree that all special and differential treatment provisions shall be reviewed with a view to strengthening them and making them more precise, effective and operational. In this

connection, we endorse the work programme on special and differential treatment set out in the Decision on Implementation-Related Issues and Concerns.

Organization and Management of the Work Programme

45. The negotiations to be pursued under the terms of this Declaration shall be concluded not later than 1 January 2005. The Fifth Session of the Ministerial Conference will take stock of progress in the negotiations, provide any necessary political guidance, and take decisions as necessary. When the results of the negotiations in all areas have been established, a Special Session of the Ministerial Conference will be held to take decisions regarding the adoption and implementation of those results.

46. The overall conduct of the negotiations shall be supervised by a Trade Negotiations Committee under the authority of the General Council. The Trade Negotiations Committee shall hold its first meeting not later than 31 January 2002. It shall establish appropriate negotiating mechanisms as required and supervise the progress of the negotiations.

47. With the exception of the improvements and clarifications of the Dispute Settlement Understanding, the conduct, conclusion and entry into force of the outcome of the negotiations shall be treated as parts of a single undertaking. However, agreements reached at an early stage may be implemented on a provisional or a definitive basis. Early agreements shall be taken into account in assessing the overall balance of the negotiations.

48. Negotiations shall be open to:

(i) all Members of the WTO; and

(ii) States and separate customs territories currently in the process of accession and those that inform Members, at a regular meeting of the General Council, of their intention to negotiate the terms of their membership and for whom an accession working party is established.

Decisions on the outcomes of the negotiations shall be taken only by WTO Members.

49. The negotiations shall be conducted in a transparent manner among participants, in order to facilitate the effective participation of all. They shall be conducted with a view to ensuring benefits to all participants and to achieving an overall balance in the outcome of the negotiations.

50. The negotiations and the other aspects of the Work Programme shall take fully into account the principle of special and differential treatment for developing and least-developed countries embodied in: Part IV of the GATT 1994; the Decision of 28 November 1979 on Differential and More Favourable Treatment, Reciprocity and Fuller Participation of Developing Countries; the Uruguay Round Decision on Measures in Favour of Least-Developed Countries; and all other relevant WTO provisions.

51. The Committee on Trade and Development and the Committee on Trade and Environment shall, within their respective mandates, each act as a forum to identify and debate developmental and environmental aspects of the negotiations, in order to help achieve the objective of having sustainable development appropriately reflected.

52. Those elements of the Work Programme which do not involve negotiations are also accorded a high priority. They shall be pursued under the overall supervision of the General Council, which shall report on progress to the Fifth Session of the Ministerial Conference.

Annexure II

Cancun Conference Ends Without Consensus

The Cancún Ministerial Conference ended on 14 September after Chairperson Luis Ernesto Derbez concluded that despite considerable movement in consultations, members remained entrenched, particularly on the "Singapore" issues.

Chairperson Derbez, who is Mexico's foreign minister, had held consultations immediately after the previous evening's heads of delegations meeting ended at about 1 am.

He described his consultations at a later meeting with all WTO members and at press conference. He said that because "speech after speech" in the heads of delegations meeting had been about the Singapore issues — trade and investment, trade and competition policy, transparency in government procurement, trade facilitation — his first consultation with a smallish group of participants had been about this group of subjects.

The consultations, which ended at about 4 am revealed that this was the most difficult issue, and he therefore decided that the next consultations, which began at about 8:30 am would start with this subject, he said.

These consultations were with a larger group representing a wide range of regional and other groups. During these consultations positions shifted, allowing the possibility of dropping negotiations on one or two subjects, Mr. Derbez said. He then suspended the consultations for transparency, so that participants could meet their respective groups.

But when the participants returned it was clear that there was no consensus and so he decided to close the meeting.

Mr. Derbez then reported to the heads of delegations meeting at about 4:00 pm. He proposed a six-paragraph ministerial statement, which was approved in the closing session at almost 6:00 pm. This instructs member governments' officials "to continue working on outstanding issues with a renewed sense of urgency and purpose and taking fully into account all the views we have expressed in this Conference."

The ministers asked the General Council Chairman and the WTO Director-General, to coordinate this work and to convene a meeting of the General Council at senior officials level no later than 15 December 2003 to take necessary action.

Director-General Supachai Panitchpakdi said there was no hiding the fact that the deadlock was a setback. He said he was disappointed but not downhearted. He said it is important to ensure the negotiations are put back on track. If the Doha Development Agenda fails, the losers will be the poor of the world, he said. He pledged to work hard for a successful outcome.

Mr. Derbez concluded that members have to learn from the lack of consensus, that business as normal will not succeed, and that some soul-searching is needed. He blamed part of the deadlock on a failure to move a way from rhetoric — no one can live off rhetoric, he said.

The WTO and its members can still make a difference for the poorest, he said.

The Ministerial Statement

1. As we conclude our Fifth Ministerial Conference in Cancún, we would like to express our deep appreciation to the Government and people of Mexico for the excellent organization and warm hospitality we have received in Cancún.

2. At this meeting we have welcomed Cambodia and Nepal as the first least-developed countries to accede to the WTO since its establishment.

3. All participants have worked hard and constructively to make progress as required under the Doha mandates. We have, indeed, made considerable progress. However, more work needs to be done in some key areas to enable us to proceed towards the conclusion of the negotiations in fulfilment of the commitments we took at Doha.

4. We therefore instruct our officials to continue working on outstanding issues with a renewed sense of urgency and purpose and taking fully into account all the views we have expressed in this Conference. We ask the Chairman of the General Council, working in close co-operation with the Director-General, to coordinate this work and to convene a meeting of the General Council at Senior Officials level no later than 15 December 2003 to take the action necessary at that stage to enable us to move towards a successful and timely conclusion of the negotiations. We shall continue to exercise close personal supervision of this process.

5. We will bring with us into this new phase all the valuable work that has been done at this Conference. In those areas where we have reached a high level of convergence on texts, we undertake to maintain this convergence while working for an acceptable overall outcome.

6. Notwithstanding this setback, we reaffirm all our Doha Declarations and Decisions and recommit ourselves to working to implement them fully and faithfully.

No Decision Yet on Next Ministerial Conference

In the closing session, the ministers asked the General Council chairperson to continue consultations on when and where the next Ministerial Conference will be held.

They noted "with appreciation" that before the General Council meeting in August, Hong Kong China had offered to host the next meeting. However, Chairperson Derbez noted that because members were preoccupied with the contents of the Cancún conference, they had not been able to discuss the dates and venue seriously, except in informal contacts with some delegations.

Decision Adopted by the General Council on 1 August 2004

1. The General Council reaffirms the Ministerial Declarations and Decisions adopted at Doha and the full commitment of all Members to give effect to them. The Council emphasizes Members' resolve to complete the Doha Work Programme fully and to conclude successfully the negotiations launched at Doha. Taking into account the Ministerial Statement adopted at Cancún on 14 September 2003, and the statements by the Council Chairman and the Director-General at the Council meeting of 15-16 December 2003, the Council takes note of the report by the Chairman of the Trade Negotiations Committee (TNC) and agrees to take action as follows:

(a) Agriculture: the General Council adopts the framework set out in Annex A to this document.

(b) Cotton: the General Council reaffirms the importance of the Sectoral Initiative on Cotton and takes note of the parameters set out in Annex A within which the trade-related aspects of this issue will be pursued in the agriculture negotiations. The General Council also attaches importance to the development aspects of the Cotton Initiative and wishes to stress the complementarity between the trade and development aspects. The Council takes note of the recent Workshop on Cotton in Cotonou on 23-24 March 2004 organized by the WTO Secretariat, and other bilateral and multilateral efforts to make progress on the development assistance aspects and instructs the Secretariat to continue to work with the development community and to provide the Council with periodic reports on relevant developments.

Members should work on related issues of development multilaterally with the international financial institutions, continue their bilateral programmes, and all developed countries are urged to participate. In this regard, the General Council instructs the Director

General to consult with the relevant international organizations, including the Bretton Woods Institutions, the Food and Agriculture Organization and the International Trade Centre to direct effectively existing programmes and any additional resources towards development of the economies where cotton has vital importance.

(c) Non-agricultural Market Access: the General Council adopts the framework set out in Annex B to this document.

(d) Development:

Principles: development concerns form an integral part of the Doha Ministerial Declaration. The General Council rededicates and recommits Members to fulfilling the development dimension of the Doha Development Agenda, which places the needs and interests of developing and least-developed countries at the heart of the Doha Work Programme. The Council reiterates the important role that enhanced market access, balanced rules, and well targeted, sustainably financed technical assistance and capacity building programmes can play in the economic development of these countries.

Special and Differential Treatment: the General Council reaffirms that provisions for special and differential (S&D) treatment are an integral part of the WTO Agreements. The Council recalls Ministers' decision in Doha to review all S&D treatment provisions with a view to strengthening them and making them more precise, effective and operational. The Council recognizes the progress that has been made so far. The Council instructs the Committee on Trade and Development in Special Session to expeditiously complete the review of all the outstanding Agreement-specific proposals and report to the General Council, with clear recommendations for a decision, by July 2005. The Council further instructs the Committee, within the parameters of the Doha mandate, to address all other outstanding work, including on the cross-cutting issues, the monitoring mechanism and the incorporation of S&D treatment into the architecture of WTO rules, as referred to in TN/CTD/7 and report, as appropriate, to the General Council.

The Council also instructs all WTO bodies to which proposals in Category II have been referred to expeditiously complete the consideration of these proposals and report to the General Council, with clear recommendations for a decision, as soon as possible and no later than July 2005. In doing so these bodies will ensure that, as far as possible, their meetings do not overlap so as to enable full and effective participation of developing countries in these discussions.

Technical Assistance: the General Council recognizes the progress that has been made since the Doha Ministerial Conference in expanding Trade-Related Technical Assistance (TRTA) to developing countries and low-income countries in transition. In furthering this effort the Council affirms that such countries, and in particular least-developed countries, should be provided with enhanced TRTA and capacity building, to increase their effective participation in the negotiations, to facilitate their implementation of WTO rules, and to enable them to adjust and diversify their economies. In this context the Council welcomes and further encourages the improved coordination with other agencies, including under the Integrated Framework for TRTA for the LDCs (IF) and the Joint Integrated Technical Assistance Programme (JITAP).

Implementation: concerning implementation-related issues, the General Council reaffirms the mandates Ministers gave in paragraph 12 of the Doha Ministerial Declaration and the Doha Decision on Implementation-Related Issues and Concerns, and renews Members' determination to find appropriate solutions to outstanding issues. The Council instructs the Trade Negotiations Committee, negotiating bodies and other WTO bodies concerned to redouble their efforts to find appropriate solutions as a priority. Without prejudice to the positions of Members, the Council requests the Director-General to continue with his consultative process on all outstanding implementation issues under paragraph 12(b) of the Doha Ministerial Declaration, including on issues related to the extension of the protection of geographical indications provided for in Article 23 of the TRIPS Agreement to products other than wines and spirits, if need be by appointing Chairpersons of concerned WTO bodies as his Friends and/or by holding dedicated consultations. The Director-General shall report to the TNC and the

General Council no later than May 2005. The Council shall review progress and take any appropriate action no later than July 2005.

Other Development Issues: in the ongoing market access negotiations, recognising the fundamental principles of the WTO and relevant provisions of GATT 1994, special attention shall be given to the specific trade and development related needs and concerns of developing countries, including capacity constraints. These particular concerns of developing countries, including relating to food security, rural development, livelihood, preferences, commodities and net food imports, as well as prior unilateral liberalisation, should be taken into consideration, as appropriate, in the course of the Agriculture and NAMA negotiations. The trade-related issues identified for the fuller integration of small, vulnerable economies into the multilateral trading system, should also be addressed, without creating a sub-category of Members, as part of a work programme, as mandated in paragraph 35 of the Doha Ministerial Declaration.

Least-Developed Countries: the General Council reaffirms the commitments made at Doha concerning least-developed countries and renews its determination to fulfil these commitments. Members will continue to take due account of the concerns of least-developed countries in the negotiations. The Council confirms that nothing in this Decision shall detract in any way from the special provisions agreed by Members in respect of these countries.

(e) Services: the General Council takes note of the report to the TNC by the Special Session of the Council for Trade in Services (1) and reaffirms Members' commitment to progress in this area of the negotiations in line with the Doha mandate. The Council adopts the recommendations agreed by the Special Session, set out in Annex C to this document, on the basis of which further progress in the services negotiations will be pursued. Revised offers should be tabled by May 2005.

(f) Other Negotiating Bodies:

Rules, Trade & Environment and TRIPS: the General Council takes note of the reports to the TNC by the Negotiating Group on Rules and by the Special Sessions of the Committee on Trade and Environment and the TRIPS Council (2). The Council reaffirms Members' commitment to progress in all of these areas of the negotiations in line with the Doha mandates.

Dispute Settlement: the General Council takes note of the report to the TNC by the Special Session of the Dispute Settlement Body (3) and reaffirms Members' commitment to progress in this area of the negotiations in line with the Doha mandate. The Council adopts the TNC's recommendation that work in the Special Session should continue on the basis set out by the Chairman of that body in his report to the TNC.

(g) Trade Facilitation: taking note of the work done on trade facilitation by the Council for Trade in Goods under the mandate in paragraph 27 of the Doha Ministerial Declaration and the work carried out under the auspices of the General Council both prior to the Fifth Ministerial Conference and after its conclusion, the General Council decides by explicit consensus to commence negotiations on the basis of the modalities set out in Annex D to this document.

Relationship between Trade and Investment, Interaction between Trade and Competition Policy and Transparency in Government Procurement: the Council agrees that these issues, mentioned in the Doha Ministerial Declaration in paragraphs 20-22, 23-25 and 26 respectively, will not form part of the Work Programme set out in that Declaration and therefore no work towards negotiations on any of these issues will take place within the WTO during the Doha Round.

(h) Other Elements of the Work Programme: the General Council reaffirms the high priority Ministers at Doha gave to those elements of the Work Programme which do not involve negotiations. Noting that a number of these issues are of particular interest to developing-country Members, the Council emphasizes its commitment to fulfil the mandates given by Ministers in all these areas. To this end, the General Council and other relevant bodies shall report in line with their Doha mandates to the Sixth Session of the Ministerial Conference. The moratoria covered by paragraph 11.1 of the Doha Ministerial

Decision on Implementation-related Issues and Concerns and paragraph 34 of the Doha Ministerial Declaration are extended up to the Sixth Ministerial Conference.

2. The General Council agrees that this Decision and its Annexes shall not be used in any dispute settlement proceeding under the DSU and shall not be used for interpreting the existing WTO Agreements.

3. The General Council calls on all Members to redouble their efforts towards the conclusion of a balanced overall outcome of the Doha Development Agenda in fulfilment of the commitments Ministers took at Doha. The Council agrees to continue the negotiations launched at Doha beyond the timeframe set out in paragraph 45 of the Doha Declaration, leading to the Sixth Session of the Ministerial Conference. Recalling its decision of 21 October 2003 to accept the generous offer of the Government of Hong Kong, China to host the Sixth Session, the Council further agrees that this Session will be held in December 2005.

ANNEX A

FRAMEWORK FOR ESTABLISHING MODALITIES IN AGRICULTURE

1. The starting point for the current phase of the agriculture negotiations has been the mandate set out in Paragraph 13 of the Doha Ministerial Declaration. This in turn built on the long-term objective of the Agreement on Agriculture to establish a fair and market-oriented trading system through a programme of fundamental reform. The elements below offer the additional precision required at this stage of the negotiations and thus the basis for the negotiations of full modalities in the next phase. The level of ambition set by the Doha mandate will continue to be the basis for the negotiations on agriculture.

2. The final balance will be found only at the conclusion of these subsequent negotiations and within the Single Undertaking. To achieve this balance, the modalities to be developed will need to incorporate operationally effective and meaningful provisions for special and

differential treatment for developing country Members. Agriculture is of critical importance to the economic development of developing country Members and they must be able to pursue agricultural policies that are supportive of their development goals, poverty reduction strategies, food security and livelihood concerns. Non-trade concerns, as referred to in Paragraph 13 of the Doha Declaration, will be taken into account.

3. The reforms in all three pillars form an interconnected whole and must be approached in a balanced and equitable manner.

4. The General Council recognizes the importance of cotton for a certain number of countries and its vital importance for developing countries, especially LDCs. It will be addressed ambitiously, expeditiously, and specifically, within the agriculture negotiations. The provisions of this framework provide a basis for this approach, as does the sectoral initiative on cotton. The Special Session of the Committee on Agriculture shall ensure appropriate prioritization of the cotton issue independently from other sectoral initiatives. A subcommittee on cotton will meet periodically and report to the Special Session of the Committee on Agriculture to review progress. Work shall encompass all trade-distorting policies affecting the sector in all three pillars of market access, domestic support, and export competition, as specified in the Doha text and this Framework text.

5. Coherence between trade and development aspects of the cotton issue will be pursued as set out in paragraph 1.b of the text to which this Framework is annexed.

Domestic Support

6. The Doha Ministerial Declaration calls for "substantial reductions in trade-distorting domestic support". With a view to achieving these substantial reductions, the negotiations in this pillar will ensure the following:

- Special and differential treatment remains an integral component of domestic support. Modalities to be developed will include longer implementation periods and lower reduction coefficients for all types of trade-distorting domestic support and continued access to the provisions under Article 6.2.

- There will be a strong element of harmonisation in the reductions made by developed Members. Specifically, higher levels of permitted trade-distorting domestic support will be subject to deeper cuts.
- Each such Member will make a substantial reduction in the overall level of its trade-distorting support from bound levels.
- As well as this overall commitment, Final Bound Total AMS and permitted *de minimis* levels will be subject to substantial reductions and, in the case of the Blue Box, will be capped as specified in paragraph 15 in order to ensure results that are coherent with the long-term reform objective. Any clarification or development of rules and conditions to govern trade distorting support will take this into account.

Overall Reduction: A Tiered Formula

7. The overall base level of all trade-distorting domestic support, as measured by the Final Bound Total AMS plus permitted *de minimis* level and the level agreed in paragraph 8 below for Blue Box payments, will be reduced according to a tiered formula. Under this formula, Members having higher levels of trade-distorting domestic support will make greater overall reductions in order to achieve a harmonizing result. As the first instalment of the overall cut, in the first year and throughout the implementation period, the sum of all trade-distorting support will not exceed 80 per cent of the sum of Final Bound Total AMS plus permitted *de minimis* plus the Blue Box at the level determined in paragraph 15.

8. The following parameters will guide the further negotiation of this tiered formula:

- This commitment will apply as a minimum overall commitment. It will not be applied as a ceiling on reductions of overall trade-distorting domestic support, should the separate and complementary formulae to be developed for Total AMS, *de minimis* and Blue Box payments imply, when taken together, a deeper cut in overall trade-distorting domestic support for an individual Member.
- The base for measuring the Blue Box component will be the higher of existing Blue Box payments during a recent representative period to be agreed and the cap established in paragraph 15 below.

Final Bound Total AMS: A Tiered Formula

9. To achieve reductions with a harmonizing effect:

- Final Bound Total AMS will be reduced substantially, using a tiered approach.
- Members having higher Total AMS will make greater reductions.
- To prevent circumvention of the objective of the Agreement through transfers of unchanged domestic support between different support categories, product-specific AMSs will be capped at their respective average levels according to a methodology to be agreed.
- Substantial reductions in Final Bound Total AMS will result in reductions of some product-specific support.

10. Members may make greater than formula reductions in order to achieve the required level of cut in overall trade-distorting domestic support.

De Minimis

11. Reductions in *de minimis* will be negotiated taking into account the principle of special and differential treatment. Developing countries that allocate almost all *de minimis* support for subsistence and resource-poor farmers will be exempt.

12. Members may make greater than formula reductions in order to achieve the required level of cut in overall trade-distorting domestic support.

Blue Box

13. Members recognize the role of the Blue Box in promoting agricultural reforms. In this light, Article 6.5 will be reviewed so that Members may have recourse to the following measures:

- Direct payments under production-limiting programmes if:
  - ☐ such payments are based on fixed and unchanging areas and yields; or
  - ☐ such payments are made on 85% or less of a fixed and unchanging base level of production; or
  - ☐ livestock payments are made on a fixed and unchanging number of head.

Or

- Direct payments that do not require production if:
  - ☐ such payments are based on fixed and unchanging bases and yields; or
  - ☐ livestock payments made on a fixed and unchanging number of head; and
  - ☐ such payments are made on 85% or less of a fixed and unchanging base level of production.

14. The above criteria, along with additional criteria will be negotiated. Any such criteria will ensure that Blue Box payments are less trade-distorting than AMS measures, it being understood that:

- Any new criteria would need to take account of the balance of WTO rights and obligations.
- Any new criteria to be agreed will not have the perverse effect of undoing ongoing reforms.

15. Blue Box support will not exceed 5% of a Member's average total value of agricultural production during an historical period. The historical period will be established in the negotiations. This ceiling will apply to any actual or potential Blue Box user from the beginning of the implementation period. In cases where a Member has placed an exceptionally large percentage of its trade-distorting support in the Blue Box, some flexibility will be provided on a basis to be agreed to ensure that such a Member is not called upon to make a wholly disproportionate cut.

Green Box

16. Green Box criteria will be reviewed and clarified with a view to ensuring that Green Box measures have no, or at most minimal, trade-distorting effects or effects on production. Such a review and clarification will need to ensure that the basic concepts, principles and effectiveness of the Green Box remain and take due account of non-trade concerns. The improved obligations for monitoring and surveillance of all new disciplines foreshadowed in paragraph 48 below will be particularly important with respect to the Green Box.

Export Competition

17. The Doha Ministerial Declaration calls for "reduction of, with a view to phasing out, all forms of export subsidies". As an outcome of the negotiations, Members agree to establish detailed modalities ensuring the parallel elimination of all forms of export subsidies and disciplines on all export measures with equivalent effect by a credible end date.

End Point

18. The following will be eliminated by the end date to be agreed:

- Export subsidies as scheduled.
- Export credits, export credit guarantees or insurance programmes with repayment periods beyond 180 days.
- Terms and conditions relating to export credits, export credit guarantees or insurance programmes with repayment periods of 180 days and below which are not in accordance with disciplines to be agreed. These disciplines will cover, inter alia, payment of interest, minimum interest rates, minimum premium requirements, and other elements which can constitute subsidies or otherwise distort trade.
- Trade distorting practices with respect to exporting STEs including eliminating export subsidies provided to or by them, government financing, and the underwriting of losses. The issue of the future use of monopoly powers will be subject to further negotiation.
- Provision of food aid that is not in conformity with operationally effective disciplines to be agreed. The objective of such disciplines will be to prevent commercial displacement. The role of international organizations as regards the provision of food aid by Members, including related humanitarian and developmental issues, will be addressed in the negotiations. The question of providing food aid exclusively in fully grant form will also be addressed in the negotiations.

19. Effective transparency provisions for paragraph 18 will be established. Such provisions, in accordance with standard WTO practice, will be consistent with commercial confidentiality considerations.

Implementation

20. Commitments and disciplines in paragraph 18 will be implemented according to a schedule and modalities to be agreed. Commitments will be implemented by annual instalments. Their phasing will take into account the need for some coherence with internal reform steps of Members.

21. The negotiation of the elements in paragraph 18 and their implementation will ensure equivalent and parallel commitments by Members.

Special and Differential Treatment

22. Developing country Members will benefit from longer implementation periods for the phasing out of all forms of export subsidies.

23. Developing countries will continue to benefit from special and differential treatment under the provisions of Article 9.4 of the Agreement on Agriculture for a reasonable period, to be negotiated, after the phasing out of all forms of export subsidies and implementation of all disciplines identified above are completed.

24. Members will ensure that the disciplines on export credits, export credit guarantees or insurance programs to be agreed will make appropriate provision for differential treatment in favour of least-developed and net food-importing developing countries as provided for in paragraph 4 of the Decision on Measures Concerning the Possible Negative Effects of the Reform Programme on Least-Developed and Net Food-Importing Developing Countries. Improved obligations for monitoring and surveillance of all new disciplines as foreshadowed in paragraph 48 will be critically important in this regard. Provisions to be agreed in this respect must not undermine the commitments undertaken by Members under the obligations in paragraph 18 above.

25. STEs in developing country Members which enjoy special privileges to preserve domestic consumer price stability and to ensure

food security will receive special consideration for maintaining monopoly status.

Special Circumstances

26. In exceptional circumstances, which cannot be adequately covered by food aid, commercial export credits or preferential international financing facilities, ad hoc temporary financing arrangements relating to exports to developing countries may be agreed by Members. Such agreements must not have the effect of undermining commitments undertaken by Members in paragraph 18 above, and will be based on criteria and consultation procedures to be established.

Market Access

27. The Doha Ministerial Declaration calls for "substantial improvements in market access". Members also agreed that special and differential treatment for developing Members would be an integral part of all elements in the negotiations.

The Single Approach: a Tiered Formula

28. To ensure that a single approach for developed and developing country Members meets all the objectives of the Doha mandate, tariff reductions will be made through a tiered formula that takes into account their different tariff structures.

29. To ensure that such a formula will lead to substantial trade expansion, the following principles will guide its further negotiation:

- Tariff reductions will be made from bound rates. Substantial overall tariff reductions will be achieved as a final result from negotiations.
- Each Member (other than LDCs) will make a contribution. Operationally effective special and differential provisions for developing country Members will be an integral part of all elements.

- Progressivity in tariff reductions will be achieved through deeper cuts in higher tariffs with flexibilities for sensitive products. Substantial improvements in market access will be achieved for all products.

30. The number of bands, the thresholds for defining the bands and the type of tariff reduction in each band remain under negotiation. The role of a tariff cap in a tiered formula with distinct treatment for sensitive products will be further evaluated.

Sensitive Products

Selection

31. Without undermining the overall objective of the tiered approach, Members may designate an appropriate number, to be negotiated, of tariff lines to be treated as sensitive, taking account of existing commitments for these products.

Treatment

32. The principle of 'substantial improvement' will apply to each product.

33. 'Substantial improvement' will be achieved through combinations of tariff quota commitments and tariff reductions applying to each product. However, balance in this negotiation will be found only if the final negotiated result also reflects the sensitivity of the product concerned.

34. Some MFN-based tariff quota expansion will be required for all such products. A base for such an expansion will be established, taking account of coherent and equitable criteria to be developed in the negotiations. In order not to undermine the objective of the tiered approach, for all such products, MFN based tariff quota expansion will be provided under specific rules to be negotiated taking into account deviations from the tariff formula.

Other Elements

35. Other elements that will give the flexibility required to reach a final balanced result include reduction or elimination of in-quota tariff rates, and operationally effective improvements in tariff quota administration for existing tariff quotas so as to enable Members, and particularly developing country Members, to fully benefit from the market access opportunities under tariff rate quotas.

36. Tariff escalation will be addressed through a formula to be agreed.

37. The issue of tariff simplification remains under negotiation.

38. The question of the special agricultural safeguard (SSG) remains under negotiation.

Special and differential treatment

39. Having regard to their rural development, food security and/or livelihood security needs, special and differential treatment for developing countries will be an integral part of all elements of the negotiation, including the tariff reduction formula, the number and treatment of sensitive products, expansion of tariff rate quotas, and implementation period.

40. Proportionality will be achieved by requiring lesser tariff reduction commitments or tariff quota expansion commitments from developing country Members.

41. Developing country Members will have the flexibility to designate an appropriate number of products as Special Products, based on criteria of food security, livelihood security and rural development needs. These products will be eligible for more flexible treatment. The criteria and treatment of these products will be further specified during the negotiation phase and will recognize the fundamental importance of Special Products to developing countries.

42. A Special Safeguard Mechanism (SSM) will be established for use by developing country Members.

43. Full implementation of the long-standing commitment to achieve the fullest liberalisation of trade in tropical agricultural products and for products of particular importance to the diversification of production from the growing of illicit narcotic crops is overdue and will be addressed effectively in the market access negotiations.

44. The importance of long-standing preferences is fully recognised. The issue of preference erosion will be addressed. For the further consideration in this regard, paragraph 16 and other relevant provisions of TN/AG/W/1/Rev.1 will be used as a reference.

Least-Developed Couontries

45. Least-Developed Countries, which will have full access to all special and differential treatment provisions above, are not required to undertake reduction commitments. Developed Members, and developing country Members in a position to do so, should provide duty-free and quota-free market access for products originating from least-developed countries.

46. Work on cotton under all the pillars will reflect the vital importance of this sector to certain LDC Members and we will work to achieve ambitious results expeditiously.

Recently Acceded Members

47. The particular concerns of recently acceded Members will be effectively addressed through specific flexibility provisions.

Monitoring and Surveillance

48. Article 18 of the Agreement on Agriculture will be amended with a view to enhancing monitoring so as to effectively ensure full transparency, including through timely and complete notifications with respect to the commitments in market access, domestic support and export competition. The particular concerns of developing countries in this regard will be addressed.

Other Issues

49 Issues of interest but not agreed: sectoral initiatives, differential export taxes, GIs.

50. Disciplines on export prohibitions and restrictions in Article 12.1 of the Agreement on Agriculture will be strengthened.

ANNEX B
FRAMEWORK FOR ESTABLISHING MODALITIES IN MARKET ACCESS FOR NON-AGRICULTURAL PRODUCTS

1. This Framework contains the initial elements for future work on modalities by the Negotiating Group on Market Access. Additional negotiations are required to reach agreement on the specifics of some of these elements. These relate to the formula, the issues concerning the treatment of unbound tariffs in indent two of paragraph 5, the flexibilities for developing-country participants, the issue of participation in the sectorial tariff component and the preferences. In order to finalize the modalities, the Negotiating Group is instructed to address these issues expeditiously in a manner consistent with the mandate of paragraph 16 of the Doha Ministerial Declaration and the overall balance therein.

2. We reaffirm that negotiations on market access for non-agricultural products shall aim to reduce or as appropriate eliminate tariffs, including the reduction or elimination of tariff peaks, high tariffs, and tariff escalation, as well as non-tariff barriers, in particular on products of export interest to developing countries. We also reaffirm the importance of special and differential treatment and less than full reciprocity in reduction commitments as integral parts of the modalities.

3. We acknowledge the substantial work undertaken by the Negotiating Group on Market Access and the progress towards achieving an agreement on negotiating modalities. We take note of the constructive dialogue on the Chair's Draft Elements of Modalities (TN/MA/W/35/Rev.1) and confirm our intention to use this document as a

reference for the future work of the Negotiating Group. We instruct the Negotiating Group to continue its work, as mandated by paragraph 16 of the Doha Ministerial Declaration with its corresponding references to the relevant provisions of Article XXVIII bis of GATT 1994 and to the provisions cited in paragraph 50 of the Doha Ministerial Declaration, on the basis set out below.

4. We recognize that a formula approach is key to reducing tariffs, and reducing or eliminating tariff peaks, high tariffs, and tariff escalation. We agree that the Negotiating Group should continue its work on a non-linear formula applied on a line-by-line basis which shall take fully into account the special needs and interests of developing and least-developed country participants, including through less than full reciprocity in reduction commitments.

5. We further agree on the following elements regarding the formula:

- product coverage shall be comprehensive without a priori exclusions;
- tariff reductions or elimination shall commence from the bound rates after full implementation of current concessions; however, for unbound tariff lines, the basis for commencing the tariff reductions shall be [two] times the MFN applied rate in the base year;
- the base year for MFN applied tariff rates shall be 2001 (applicable rates on 14 November);
- credit shall be given for autonomous liberalization by developing countries provided that the tariff lines were bound on an MFN basis in the WTO since the conclusion of the Uruguay Round;
- all non-*ad valorem* duties shall be converted to *ad valorem* equivalents on the basis of a methodology to be determined and bound in *ad valorem* terms;
- negotiations shall commence on the basis of the HS96 or HS2002 nomenclature, with the results of the negotiations to be finalized in HS2002 nomenclature;

- the reference period for import data shall be 1999-2001.

6. We furthermore agree that, as an exception, participants with a binding coverage of non-agricultural tariff lines of less than [35] percent would be exempt from making tariff reductions through the formula. Instead, we expect them to bind [100] percent of non-agricultural tariff lines at an average level that does not exceed the overall average of bound tariffs for all developing countries after full implementation of current concessions.

7. We recognize that a sectorial tariff component, aiming at elimination or harmonization is another key element to achieving the objectives of paragraph 16 of the Doha Ministerial Declaration with regard to the reduction or elimination of tariffs, in particular on products of export interest to developing countries. We recognize that participation by all participants will be important to that effect. We therefore instruct the Negotiating Group to pursue its discussions on such a component, with a view to defining product coverage, participation, and adequate provisions of flexibility for developing-country participants.

8. We agree that developing-country participants shall have longer implementation periods for tariff reductions. In addition, they shall be given the following flexibility:

a) applying less than formula cuts to up to [10] percent of the tariff lines provided that the cuts are no less than half the formula cuts and that these tariff lines do not exceed [10] percent of the total value of a Member's imports; or
b) keeping, as an exception, tariff lines unbound, or not applying formula cuts for up to [5] percent of tariff lines provided they do not exceed [5] percent of the total value of a Member's imports.

We furthermore agree that this flexibility could not be used to exclude entire HS Chapters.

9. We agree that least-developed country participants shall not be required to apply the formula nor participate in the sectorial approach, however, as part of their contribution to this round of negotiations,

they are expected to substantially increase their level of binding commitments.

10. Furthermore, in recognition of the need to enhance the integration of least-developed countries into the multilateral trading system and support the diversification of their production and export base, we call upon developed-country participants and other participants who so decide, to grant on an autonomous basis duty-free and quota-free market access for non-agricultural products originating from least-developed countries by the year [...].

11. We recognize that newly acceded Members shall have recourse to special provisions for tariff reductions in order to take into account their extensive market access commitments undertaken as part of their accession and that staged tariff reductions are still being implemented in many cases. We instruct the Negotiating Group to further elaborate on such provisions.

12. We agree that pending agreement on core modalities for tariffs, the possibilities of supplementary modalities such as zero-for-zero sector elimination, sectorial harmonization, and request & offer, should be kept open.

13. In addition, we ask developed-country participants and other participants who so decide to consider the elimination of low duties.

14. We recognize that NTBs are an integral and equally important part of these negotiations and instruct participants to intensify their work on NTBs. In particular, we encourage all participants to make notifications on NTBs by 31 October 2004 and to proceed with identification, examination, categorization, and ultimately negotiations on NTBs. We take note that the modalities for addressing NTBs in these negotiations could include request/offer, horizontal, or vertical approaches; and should fully take into account the principle of special and differential treatment for developing and least-developed country participants.

15. We recognize that appropriate studies and capacity building measures shall be an integral part of the modalities to be agreed. We also recognize the work that has already been undertaken in these areas

and ask participants to continue to identify such issues to improve participation in the negotiations.

16. We recognize the challenges that may be faced by non-reciprocal preference beneficiary Members and those Members that are at present highly dependent on tariff revenue as a result of these negotiations on non-agricultural products. We instruct the Negotiating Group to take into consideration, in the course of its work, the particular needs that may arise for the Members concerned.

17. We furthermore encourage the Negotiating Group to work closely with the Committee on Trade and Environment in Special Session with a view to addressing the issue of non-agricultural environmental goods covered in paragraph 31 (iii) of the Doha Ministerial Declaration.

ANNEX C

RECOMMENDATIONS OF THE SPECIAL SESSION OF THE COUNCIL FOR TRADE IN SERVICES

(a) Members who have not yet submitted their initial offers must do so as soon as possible.

(b) A date for the submission of a round of revised offers should be established as soon as feasible.

(c) With a view to providing effective market access to all Members and in order to ensure a substantive outcome, Members shall strive to ensure a high quality of offers, particularly in sectors and modes of supply of export interest to developing countries, with special attention to be given to least-developed countries.

(d) Members shall aim to achieve progressively higher levels of liberalization with no a priori exclusion of any service sector or mode of supply and shall give special attention to sectors and modes of supply of export interest to developing countries. Members note the interest of developing countries, as well as other Members, in Mode 4.

(e) Members must intensify their efforts to conclude the negotiations on rule-making under GATS Articles VI:4, X, XIII and XV in accordance with their respective mandates and deadlines.

(f) Targeted technical assistance should be provided with a view to enabling developing countries to participate effectively in the negotiations.

(g) For the purpose of the Sixth Ministerial meeting, the Special Session of the Council for Trade in Services shall review progress in these negotiations and provide a full report to the Trade Negotiations Committee, including possible recommendations.

ANNEX D
ODALITIES FOR NEGOTIATIONS ON TRADE FACILITATION

1. Negotiations shall aim to clarify and improve relevant aspects of Articles V, VIII and X of the GATT 1994 with a view to further expediting the movement, release and clearance of goods, including goods in transit (4). Negotiations shall also aim at enhancing technical assistance and support for capacity building in this area. The negotiations shall further aim at provisions for effective cooperation between customs or any other appropriate authorities on trade facilitation and customs compliance issues.

2. The results of the negotiations shall take fully into account the principle of special and differential treatment for developing and least-developed countries. Members recognize that this principle should extend beyond the granting of traditional transition periods for implementing commitments. In particular, the extent and the timing of entering into commitments shall be related to the implementation capacities of developing and least-developed Members. It is further agreed that those Members would not be obliged to undertake investments in infrastructure projects beyond their means.

3. Least-developed country Members will only be required to undertake commitments to the extent consistent with their individual development, financial and trade needs or their administrative and institutional capabilities.

4. As an integral part of the negotiations, Members shall seek to identify their trade facilitation needs and priorities, particularly those of developing and least-developed countries, and shall also address the concerns of developing and least-developed countries related to cost implications of proposed measures.

5. It is recognized that the provision of technical assistance and support for capacity building is vital for developing and least-developed countries to enable them to fully participate in and benefit from the negotiations. Members, in particular developed countries, therefore commit themselves to adequately ensure such support and assistance during the negotiations (5).

6. Support and assistance should also be provided to help developing and least-developed countries implement the commitments resulting from the negotiations, in accordance with their nature and scope. In this context, it is recognized that negotiations could lead to certain commitments whose implementation would require support for infrastructure development on the part of some Members. In these limited cases, developed-country Members will make every effort to ensure support and assistance directly related to the nature and scope of the commitments in order to allow implementation. It is understood, however, that in cases where required support and assistance for such infrastructure is not forthcoming, and where a developing or least-developed Member continues to lack the necessary capacity, implementation will not be required. While every effort will be made to ensure the necessary support and assistance, it is understood that the commitments by developed countries to provide such support are not open-ended.

7. Members agree to review the effectiveness of the support and assistance provided and its ability to support the implementation of the results of the negotiations.

8. In order to make technical assistance and capacity building more effective and operational and to ensure better coherence, Members shall invite relevant international organizations, including the IMF, OECD, UNCTAD, WCO and the World Bank to undertake a collaborative effort in this regard.

9. Due account shall be taken of the relevant work of the WCO and other relevant international organizations in this area.

10. Paragraphs 45-51 of the Doha Ministerial Declaration shall apply to these negotiations. At its first meeting after the July session of the General Council, the Trade Negotiations Committee shall establish a Negotiating Group on Trade Facilitation and appoint its Chair. The first meeting of the Negotiating Group shall agree on a work plan and schedule of meeting

Bibliography

ADB. 1999, *Asian Development Outlook* 1999, Hong Kong: Oxford University Press (for the Asian Development Bank. Manila).

ADB. 2000, *Asian Development Outlook 2000,* Hong Kong: Oxford University Press (for the Asian Development Bank. Manila).

ADB. 2001a, *Asian Development Outlook 2001,* Hong Kong: Oxford University Press (for the Asian Development Bank:, Manila).

ADB. 2001b, *Asian Development Outlook Update,* November. Manila: Asian Development Bank.

ADB Institute. 2000, *Policy Recommendations for Preventing Another Capita/Account Crisis.* Asian Policy Forum. Tokyo: ADB Institute.

Adhikari. R. 2000, "Agreement on Agriculture and food Security: South Asian Perspective". *South Asia Economic Journal.* 2(1), September, 43-65.

Ahmed, S. 1999, *Star Magazine,* Colombo. 2 July.

Ahluwalia, *S.S.* 1998, Paper presented at the South Asia Energy Symposium on *Energy-Policies of South Asian Nations Toward the* 21 *Century,* Tokyo, Ministry of Foreign Affairs of Japan, 27 February.

Akhtar, S. and F. Malik. 2000, Pakistan's Trade Performance vis-a-vis Its Major Trading Partners. *Pakistan Development Review,* 39(1) Spring: 37-50.

Ariff, Mohammed. 1999, "The Financial Crisis and the Reshaping of the Malaysian Economy: Trends and Issues. *Eighth Indian-ASEAN Eminent Person Lecture.* 'New Delhi: Research and Information System for the Non-Aligned and Other Developing Countries.

Asthana, S.; 2000, "A Tight Squeeze", *Business Standard, 4* September.

ATIP. 1998. Software Activities in Pakistan, Asian Technology Information Programme, http://www.atip.org.

AT Keamey. 2001, *FDI Confidence Index.* Global Business Policy Council, February. http://www.atkeamey.com

Athukorala, P. and S. Rajapatirana, 2000, *Liberalization and industrial Transformation.* Delhi: Oxford University Press.

Bagchi, I, 2000, Indo-Iran Gas Panel Stumbles on Security, *The Economic Times. 23* August.

Bakht, Z. 2000. "Growth Performance of the Manufacturing Sector: A Review of the Revised Industrial GDP under SNA 93, Dhaka: Bangladesh Institute of Development Studies, November (mimeo).

Bangladesh, Ministry of Finance. 1999, *Bangladesh Economic Review,* 1999, Dhaka.

Bangladesh, Ministry of Finance. 2000, *Bangladesh Economic Review* 2000, Dhaka.

Bangladesh, Ministry of Finance. 2001, *Action Programme for the Development of Bangladesh, 2001-2010.* Country Presentation of the Government of Bangladesh at the Third UN Conference on the Least Developed Countries. Brussels. 14-20 May.

Banerjee, S. and S. Mukherjee, 2000, No Takers for AES Power, *The Economic Times TJ* August. Bhattacharya, D., et al. 2000. A Preliminary Note on the New National Income Estimates, *The Independent*, 30 April.

Bhattacharya, S.K, 2001, regional Trading Arrangements among SAARC Countries: Do They Increase India's Imports? *South Asia Economic Journal.* 2(2), July-December.

Bhutan, Ministry of Finance, 2001, *Action Programme for the Development of Bhutan, 2001-2010.* Country Presentation of the Royal Government of Bhutan at the Third UN Conference on the Least Developed Countries, Brussels, 14-20 May.

Bhutan, Royal Monetary Authority of. 2000a. *Selected Economic Indicators.* 14 (3), Thimpu: Royal Monetary Authority of Bhutan, September.

Bhutan, Royal Monetary Authority of. 2000b. *Selected Economic Indicators*. 14 (4), Thimpu: Royal Monetary Authority of Bhutan, December.

Bhutan, Royal Monetary Authority of. 200la. *Selected Economic Indicators*, 15 (1), Thimpu: Royal Monetary Authority of Bhutan, March.

Bhutan, Royal Monetary Authority of. 2001b. *Selected Economic Indicators*. 15 (2)., Thimpu: Royal Monetary Authority of Bhutan, June.

Bokhari, F/1998, "South Asian Software", *The Financial Times*, 1 July.

Bokhari, F. 1999, "South Asian Software and Services", *Financial Times Survey*. 2 June.

Brahmbhatt, M., T.G. Srinivasan and K. Murrell, 1996, "India in the Global Economy", *Policy Research Working Paper* 1681, International Economic Analysis and Prospects Division. Washington D.C.: The World Bank.

Brenner, C. 1998, "Intellectual Property Rights and Technology Transfer in Developing Country Agriculture: Rhetoric and Reality." *OECD, Technical Paper No*. 133. Paris: OECD.

Business India. 1999, 20 September 3-October, 104-110.

Business Standard. 2001, CII Says Indo-Lanka FTA has more Opportunities than Threats, A Sponsored Supplement", 25 January.

Cecchini, P. 1988, The European Challenge: 1992: The Benefits of a Single Market, *Aldershot: Wildwood House*.

Central Bank of Sri Lanka. 2000, *Annual Report 2000*, Colombo: Central Bank of Sri Lanka.

Chettri, P.B. and R. Shrestha. 2000, *Problems and Prospect of Power Sector in Nepal, Paper* prepared for Centre for Economic Development and Administration, Tribhuwan University, Kathmandu.

Crishna, V. et al. 1999, Telecommunications Infrastructure, *Economic and Political Weekly*, 20 November.

Colombage, S.S. (ed.). 1998, *Opportunities for Trade and Investment Expansion for Sri Lanka under SAPTA and SAFTA, EES* Publication 30, Friedrich Ebert Stiftung, Colombo.

Dahal, M.K.(ed.). 1999, *Impact of Globalization in Nepal,* Kathmandu; 'Nepal Foundation for Advanced Studies (NEFAS) & Friedrich-Ebert-Stiftung.

Dasgupta, A. 2000, "Labour Standards and WTO: A New Form of Protectionism," *South Asia Economic Journal.* 2(1),' September, 113-129.

Datt, G. 1999, "Has Poverty Declined since Economic Reforms?" *Economic and Political Weekly,* 34 (50): 3516-28.

Deraniyagala, A 1998, Paper presented at the South Asia Energy Symposium on *Energy Policies of South Asian Nations, Towards the 21st century,* Tokyo, Muustry ofForiegn Affairs, 27 February.

DeRosa, D. A 1995, "Regional Trading Arrangements Among Developing Countries: The ASEAN Example" *Research Report 103,* Washington D.C: International Food Policy Research Institute.

Dhar, B. 1998. "Complying, in the TRIPs Commitment: EMRs vs Product Patents, *Economic and Political Weekly,* 19 December.

Dhar, B. 1999. The GATT Agreement on Agriculture and Its Impact on Indian Agriculture, *Asia Pacific Research Journal, December.*

Dhar, B. 2001, "The Non-Trade Concerns in the Agreement on Agriculture", *Occasional Paper No. 60.* New Delhi: Research and Information System for the Non-Aligned and Other Developing Countries.

Dhar, B. and S. Chaturvedi. 1998, "Multilateral Agreement on Investment: An Analysis" *Economic and Political Weekly,* 11 April.

Dhar, B. and S. Chaturvedi. 1999. *WTO Agreement and Agricultural Sector: Implications and Options for India, New* Delhi: RIS.

Dhar, B., S. Chaturvedi. and R.V. Anuradha, 2001, *Regime of Intellectual Property Protection for Biodiversity: A Developing Country Perspective,* New Delhi: RIS and MCN.

Dubey, M., L.R. Baral and R. Sobhan (ed.). 1999, *South Asian Growth Quadrangle: Framework for Multifaceted Coopeation,* New Delhi: Macmillan India Limited.

Dubey, M. and N. Jetly (ed.). 1999, *South Asia and Its Eastern Neighbours, Building a Relationship in the 21st Century,* New Delhi: Friedrich Ebert Stiftung.

Dunning, J.H. 1993, *Multinational Enterprises and the Global Economy, Reading*: Addison-Wesley.

Dunning, J.H., 1998, The Changing Geography of Foreign Direct Investment", in N. Kumar et al. *Globalization, Foreign Direct Investment and Technology Transfer: Impact on and Prospects for Developing Countries*. London: Routledge. 43-90.

ECS, 1999, *Indian Software, A Story of Unparalleled Success,* New Delhi: Electronics and Computer Software Export Promotion Council.

Einarsson, P., 2001, The Disagreement on Agriculture, *Seedling*. March. 5.

Elena, S. P., Jose Antonio, N. P. and Jose, M.N., 1999, Endogenous Preferential Trade Agreements. *Journal of Economic Integration,* 14 (3). September. 419-431.

ESCAP, 1996, *The Role of the Private Sector and Privatization for Industrial and Technological Development in South Asian Economies, New* York: United Nations.

ESCAP, 1997a, *BIST-EC Development Programme: Overview and Sectoral Cooperation,* New York: United Nations.

ESCAP, 1997b, *Regional Action Plan for Implementation of the New Delhi Action Plan on Infrastructure Development in Asia and the Pacific*, New York: United Nations. York: United Nations.

ESCAP, 1998, "Enhancement of Trade and Investment Cooperation in South-east Asia: Opportunities and Challenges Toward ASEAN-10 and Beyond", *Studies in Trade and Investment,* 34, New

ESCAP, 1999a, *Implications of the Asian Crisis on Sustainable Industrial and Technological Development in the AsiaPacific Region,* New York: United Nations.

ESCAP, 1999c, *Utilizing Industrial Complementarities in an Era of the Open Regionalism*, New York: United Nations

ESCAP, 1999A, "Trade and Investment Scenarios and Liberalization Agenda for Asia and the Pacific", *Studies in Trade and Investment 36,* New York: United Nations.

ESCAP, 1999e, *Economic and Social Survey of Asia and the Pacific 1999,* Bangkok: UN-ESCAP.

ESCAP, 1999f, *Country Background Paper for the Economic and Social Survey: Bhutan,* Bangkok: UN-ESCAP. (mimeo.)

ESCAP, 1999g, *Country Background Paper for the Economic and Social Survey: Pakistan,* Bangkok: UN-ESCAP. (mimeo.)

ESCAP, 2000, *Economic and Social Survey of Asia and the Pacific 2000,* Bangkok: United Nations.

ESCAP, 2001, *Economic and Social Survey of Asia and the Pacific, 20011,* New York: United Nations.

FAO. 1998, *Production Yearbook* 1998, Rome: Food and Agriculture Organisation.

FAO. 1999, *Production Yearbook* 1999, Rome: Food and Agriculture Organisation.

FNCCI. 2000, *Nepal and The World A Statistical Profile 2000,* Katmandu. Federation of Nepalese Chambers of Commerce & Industry.

Ghafoor, A and J. Weiss. 1999, "Privatisation of Electric Power Sector in Pakistan: Some Important Issues", *Pakistan Development Review,* 38(1), Spring, 6984.

Goyal, A. 2000, "Reform Proposals from Developing Asia: Finding a Win-Win Strategy", *Working Paper,*

Mumbai. Indira Gandhi Institute of Development Research.

Guha, S. 2000, "The Politics of Energy", *The Times of India,* August 18.

Hanson, A. and S. Kathuria (eds.). 1999, *India: A Financial Sector for the Twenty-first Century,* New Delhi: Oxford University Press for the World Bank.

Haq, E. 2000, "Exxon Mobil Winding Up in Bangladesh", *The Economic Times,* 14 September.

Harilal, K. N., and Joseph, K. J. 1999, "IndiaSri Lanka Free Trade Accord, *Economic and Political Weekly,* 27 March.

HDC. 1999, *Human Development in South Asia,* Karachi: Oxford University Press (for the Mahbub-ul Haq Human Development Centre).

HDC. 2000, *Human Development in South Asia,* Karachi: Oxford University Press (for the Mahbub-ul Haq Human Development Centre).

HDC. 2001, *Human Development in South Asia,* Karachi: Oxford University Press (for the Mahbub-ul Haq Human Development Centre).

Hertel, T. W., C. F. Bach, B. Dimaranan and W. Martin. 1996, "Growth, Globalization, and Gains from the Uruguay Round", *Policy Research Working Paper* 1614. International Economics Department, International Trade Di vision, Washington D.C.: The World Bank.

Hoekman, Bernard. 1993, "Developing Countries and the Uruguay Round: Negotiations on Services", *Policy Research Working Paper 1220,* Europe and Central Asia, and Middle East and North Africa Regions Technical Department Finance and Private Sector Development Division,'Washington D.C.; The World Bank.

Hussain, S. T. 1998, Paper presented at the South Asia Energy Symposium on *Energy Policies of South Asian Nations Toward the 21st Century,* Tokyo: Ministry of Foreign Affairs of Japan., 27 February.

Hyder, G. 1998, Paper presented at the South Asia Energy Symposium on *Energy Policies of South Asian Nations Toward the 21st Century,* Tokyo: Ministry of Foreign Affairs of Japan., 27 February.

Ikram. T. 2000, *The Economic Times. AS* June. IMF. 2000, *World Economic Outlook.* October 2000. Washngton DC: International Monetary Fund.

IMF. 2001a, *World Economic Outlook,* May 2001. Washington D.C.: International Monetary Fund.

IMF. 2001b, *World Economic Outlook,* October 2001. Washington D.C.: International Monetary Fund.

India, Indian Investment Centre. 1999, *Indian Joint Ventures and Wholly Owned Subsidiaries Abroad Approved During the year* 1999, New Delhi: Indian Investment Centre.

India, Ministry of External Affairs. 1998, *Discover India.* As available in www. meadev. gov.inlforeignlsaarc.htm.

India, Ministry of External Affairs. 2000, *Discover India.* As available in www. meadev. gov.inlforeignlbhutan.htm

India, Ministry of Finance. 1999, *Economic Survey* 1998/99, New Delhi: Government of India.

India, Ministry of Finance. 2000, *Economic Survey 1999/2000,* New Delhi: Government of India.

India, Ministry of Finance, 2001, *Economic Survey 2000/01*, New Delhi: Government of India.

Islam, N. 2001, "South Asia and World Economy: Challenges Ahead", in W. Mahmud (ed.), *Adjustment and Beyond: The Reform Experience in South Asia*, Hampshire: Palgrave (in association with International E India, Ministry of Petroleum and Natural Gas. 1999. *Indian Petroleum and Natural Gas Statistics*. New Delhi: Government of India.

Infolink PC World. 1999, Colombo. October.

IPS. 1999, *Sri Lanka: State of the Economy*, 1999, October. Colombo: Institute of Policy Studies.

IPS. 2000, *Sri Lanka: State of the Economy 2000*, October. Colombo: Institute of Policy Studies.

Islam, N. 2001, "South Asia and World Economy: Challenges Ahead", in W. Mahmud (ed.). *Adjustment and Beyond: The Reform Experience in South Asia*, Hampshire: Palgrave (in association with International Economic Association). 307-13.Economic Association). 307-13.

ITC/Commonwealth Secretariat. 1996, *A Business Guide to Uruguay Round Agreements*. Geneva: International Trade Centre.

Jayasuria, L. 2001, "Rethinking Social Development: Towards an Equitable Future for Sri Lanka", *South Asia Economic Journal*. 2(1), January-June, 105-121.

Jha, H.B. (ed.). 1995, *Duty-free Border Trade and Special Economic Zone between Nepal and India*. Kathmandu: Centre for Economic and Technical Studies in cooperation with Friedrich Ebert Stiftung.

Jorgenson, D. W. and K. J. Stiroh. 2000, "Raising the Speed Limit: US Economic Growth in the Information Age" in *Economic Activity 1:2000*, Washington D.C.: Brookings Institution, 125-235.

Joshi, G. (ed.). 2000, *Privatization in South Asia: Minimizing Negative Social Effects Through Restructuring*. New Delhi: International Labour Organization-SAAT.

Karmacharya, B. K. 2001, "Economic Reforms in Nepal and Their Implications for Trade, Economic Growth, Inequality and Poverty", *South Asia Economic Journal*. 2(1) January-June, 87-103.

Katti, V. 1995, "Duty Free Border Trade and Specific Economic Zone between India and Nepal" in H.B. Jha (ed.). *Duty-free Border Trade and Special Economic Zone between Nepal and India.* Kathmandu: Centre for Economic and Technical Studies in cooperation with Friedrich Ebert Stiftung.

Kaur, H. 2001, "Get Asian Fund Going Fast", *Third World Resurgence,* 127/128. Marchi April.

Kelegama, S. 1998, "Economic Development in Sri Lanka during the 50 Years of Independence: What Went Wrong?" *Occasional Paper No.* 53, New Delhi: Research and Information System for the Non-Aligned and Other Developing Countries.

Kelegama, S. 1999, "Indo-Sri Lanka Trade and the Bilateral Free Trade Agreement: A Sri Lankan Perspective," *Asia-Pacific Development Journal, 6* (2), December.

Kelegama, S. et al. 2000, Foreign Direct Investment and Economic Integration in the SAARC Region. *Report submitted to SANE!. Colombo: Institute of Policy Studies.*

Kemal, A. R. 1999, "Patterns and Growth of Pakistan's Industrial Sector" in S.R. Khan, (ed.), *Fifty Years of Pakistan's Economic: Traditional Topics and Contemporary Concerns.* Karachi: Oxford University Press, 155-157.

Kemal, A. R. 2001, "Structural adjustment. Employment and Poverty in Pakistan" in W. Mahmud (ed.), *Adjustment and Beyond: The Reform Experience in South Asia* Hampshire: Palgrave (in association with International Economic Association). 63-73.

Khan, A. H. 1997, "Foreign Direct Investment in Pakistan: Policies and Trends", *Pakistan Development* Review, 36. *959-985.*

Khan, A. H. 1998, "The Experience of Trade Liberalization in Pakistan", *Pakistan Development Review,. 37* (4). 661-685.

Khondker, B.H. and A.H. Chaudhury. 2001, "Growth with Equity: A Bangladesh Perspective", *South Asia Economic Journal.* 2(1): January-June. 67-86.

Khor, M. 2000, "Globalization and the South: Some Critical Issues", *UNCTAD Working Paper No. 147.* Geneva.

Klein, L. R. 2000, "Sustainability of Economic Expansion in the United States", Keynote Speech delivered at the Workshop on External

Environment and Sustainability of the East Asian Recovery, Tokyo: ADB Institute, 4 September.

Kumar. N. 1986, "Foreign Direct Investment and Technology Transfers among Developing Countries" in V. R. Panchamukhi et. al., *The Third World and the World Economic System,* New Delhi: Radiant Publishers, pp. 139-165.

Kumar, N. 1992, "Resource Flows and Foreign Direct Investments in Developing Countries: Trends and Prospects", *RIS Digest.* 9 (3), September, pp. 43-56.

Kumar. N. 1998a, "Multinational Enterprises, Regional Economic Integration and Export Platform Production in the Host Countries: An Empirical Analysis for the US and Japanese Corporations" *WeltwirtschaftlichesArchiv,* 134 (3): 450483.

Kumar, N. 1998b, "Liberalisation and Changing Patterns of Foreign Direct Investments: Has India's Relative Attractiveness as a Host of FDI Improved?", *Economic and Political Weekly.* 30 May; 1321-29.

Kumar, N. 1998c, *Globalisation Foreign Direct Investment and Technology Transfers. Impacts on Prospects for Developing Countries,* London and New York: Routledge.

Kumar, N. (ed.). *2000a, Indian Economy under Reforms: An Assessment of Economic and Social Impact.* New Delhi: Bookwell (for Research and Information System for the Non-Aligned and Other Developing Countries).

Kumar, N. 2000b, "Explaining the Geography and Depth of International Production: The Case of US and Japanese Multinational Enterprises", *WeltwirtschaftlichesArchiv,* 136(3): 442-476.

Kumar, N. 2001a, "Flying Geese Theory and Japanese Foreign Direct Investment in South Asia: Trends Explanations and future Prospects," *Journal of International Economic Studies,* 15: 179192.

Kumar, N. 2001b, "Foreign Direct Investment, Regional Economic Integration and Industrial Restructuring in Asia: Trends, Patterns and Prospects", *Occasional Paper No.* 62. New Delhi: Research and Information System for the Non-Aligned and Other Developing Countries.

Kumar, N. 2001c. "*WTOs* Emerging Investment Regime and Developing Countries: The Way Forward for TRIMs Review and the Doha Ministerial Meeting", *Discussion Paper* 14. New Delhi: Research and Information System for the Non-Aligned and Other Developing Countries.

Kumar, N. 2001d, "IDdian Software Industry Development in International and National Development Perspective". *Discussion Paper* 19-New Delhi: Research and Information System for the Non-Aligned and Other Developing Countries.

Kumar, N. 2001e, "National Innovation Systems and the Indian Software Industry Development," A Background Paper for the *World Industrial Development Report 2002,* Vienna: UNIDO.

Kumar, N. 2002, *Globalisation and Quality of FDI: A Quantitative Analysis of the Role of Host Country Characteristics and WTO Regime.* Delhi: Oxford University Press (forthcoming).

Kumar, N. and N. S. Siddharthan. 1997, *Technology, Market Structure and Internationalization-Issues and Policies for Developing Countries.* UNU/INTECH Studies in New Technology and Development. London and New Yark: Routfedge.

Kwa, A. 2001, "WTO Agriculture Negotiations: US' Arrognace, EU's Hypocrisy and Developing Countries Weaknesses on Parade", in www.wlowatch.org

Lakshman, W. D. (ed.). 1997, *Dilemmas of Development: Fifty Years of Economic Change in Sri Lanka,* Colombo: Sri Lanka Association of Economists. Lall, S. 1999, "India's Manufactured Exports: Comparative Structure and Prospects". *World Development.* 27(10): 1769-86.

Lall, S. 2000, "The Technological Structure and Performance of Developing Country Manufactured Exports, 1985-1998", Oxford: University of Oxford International Development Centre (mimeographed).

Lama, M. P. 1999a, "Economic Reforms and Energy Sector in South Asia: Scope for Cross Border Power Trade", Paper presented at the SAARC Seminar: *Improving Infrastructure in the Energy, Transport and Communications Sector.* 10-11 December. New Delhi: India International Centre, Indian Council South Asian Cooperation and TERI.

Lama, M. P. 1999b, Integrated Programme of Action in SAARC: Genesis, Evaluation, Constraints and Rationale for Revamping, *Occasional Paper No* 57, New Delhi: Research and Information System for the Non-Aligned and Other Developing Countries.

Lama, M. P. and R. B. Rais. 2001, *Pipelines and Powergrids for Peace*. Mumbai: International Centre for Peace Iniciatives.

Latheef, M. 1998, Paper presented at the South Asia Energy Symposium on *Energy Policies of South Asian Nations Toward the 21st Century*, Tokyo: Ministry of Foreign Affairs of Japan, 27 February.

Lipsey, R. G. 1970, *The Theory of Customs Union: A General Equilibrium Analysis*. London: Westfield and Nicolson.

Loayza, N. and R. Shankar. 2000, "Private Saving in India". *World Bank Economic Review*. 14(3): 571-94.

Mahendra Dev, S. 2000, "Poverty, Income Distribution and Employment Under Reforms", in N. Kumar (ed.), *Indian Economy Under Reforms: An Assessment of Economic and Social Impact*. New Delhi: Bookwell (for the Research and Information System for the Non-Aligned and Other Developing Countries). 93-150.

Mahmud, W. 2001a, "Bangladesh: Structural Adjustment and Beyond," in W. Mahmud (ed.) *Adjustment and Beyond: The Reform Experience in South Asia*. Hampshire: Palgrave.

Mahmud, W. (ed.). 2001b, *Adjustment and Beyond: The Reform Experience in South Asia*, Hampshire: Palgrave (in association with International Economic Association).

Majd, N. 1995, "The Uruguay Round and South Asia: An Overview of the Impact and Opportunities." *Policy Research Working Paper No*. 1484, International Economics Department, International Trade Vision. Washington, D.C: The World Bank.

Mahapatra, R. 2000, "Power the People", *Down to Earth*. 30 November: 31-40.

Maldives, Ministry of Planning. 1998, *Fifth National Development Plan. 1997-2000*. Male: The Government of the Republic of The Maldives.

Mansell, R. and U. Wehn (eds). 1998, *Knowledge Societies: Information Technology for Sustainable Development*. New York: Oxford University Press for the United Nations.

Maskay, N. M. 2001, "South Asian Monetary Integration in the Light of the Optimum Currency Area Criterion of Patterns of Shocks". *South Asia Economic Journal.* 2(2). July-December.

Mayer, J. and A. Wood. 2000, "South Asia's Export Structure in a Comparative Perspective", *IDS Working Paper* 91. Sussex: Institute for Development Studies.

Meade, J. E. 1955, *The Theory of Customs Unions.* Amsterdam: North-Holland.

Mehta, A. and Akhtar, S. 1999, "Promoting the Internet in South Asia". *Economic and Political Weekly.* 20 November.

Mehta, D. 1999, "Non-tariff Barriers in FT Trade: Experience of India", Presentation at the WTO Information Technology Symposium, Geneva, 16 July.

Mehta, P.S. and U. Kunaar. 2000, 'Trade, Competition Policy & International Competition Rules: A South Asian Perspective", *South Asia Economic Journal.* 2(1). September. 65-94.

Mehta, R 1999, *Tariff and Non-tariff Barriers of Indian Economy A Profile,* New Delhi: Research and Information System for the Non-Aligned and Other Developing Countries.

Mehta, R and S.K. Mohanty. 1999, *WTO and Industrial Tariffs: An Empirical Analysis for India.* New Delhi: Research and Information System for the Non-Aligned and Other Developing Countries.

Mehta, R. 2000, *QR Removal and India's Import: The Case of India's Unilateral Offer for SAARC Countries.* New Delhi: Research and Information System for the Non-Aligned and Other Developing Countries.

Mehta, R. 2001, *"WTO, Liberalisation and Industrial Sector: The Case of Market Access",* Occasional Paper No. 63, New Delhi: Research and Information System for the Non-Aligned and Other Developing Countries.

Mehta, R. and S. K. Bhattacharya. 1999, "The South Asian Preferential Trading Arrangement: Impact on Intra-Regional Trade". *Asia Pacific Journal,* 4(1): 92111.

Mehta, V.S. 2000, "South Asian Forum for Energy Development", *The Economic Times,* August 19.

Mishra, Land C.D. Wadhwa 1991, "Regional Cooperation in Industry and Energy, Prospects for South Asia" in Waqif, A.A. (ed.) *Regional Cooperation in Industry and Energy, Prospects for South Asia.* New Delhi: Sage: 197-213.

Mohan, R 1999, Economic Reforms: The Next Wave, Lalit Doshi Memorial Lecture, 30 August.

Moran, T. H. 1998, *Foreign Direct Investment and Development.* Washington D.C.: Institute for International Economics.

Mukherjee, I. N. 1998, India's Trade and Investment Languages with Nepal: Some Reflections. *South Asian Survey.* 5(2): 183-97.

Mukherjee, I. N. 2000, "Indo-Sri Lanka Trade and Investment Linkages: With Special Reference to SAPT A and Free Trade Agreement", *South Asia Economic Journal,* 1(1). March: 53-77.

Mukherjee, N. 2000, *World Trade Organization and India's Trade Policy in Services,* New Delhi: Vikas Publishing House Pvt. Ltd.

Muni, S. D. 1992, *India and Nepal: The Changing Relationship.* New Delhi: Konark Publishing Pvt. Ltd.

Musleh-Ud Din and K. Abbas. 2000, "The Uruguay Round Agreement and Pakistan's Trade in Textiles and Clothing." *South Asia Economic Journal,* 1(1): 101-15.

March. Mytelka, L. K. (ed.). 1992, *South-South Cooperation in a Global Perspective.* Paris: Organisation for Economic Cooperation and Development.

NASSCOM. 2000, *The I.T. Software and Services Industry in India: Strategic Review 2000,* New Delhi: National Association of Software and Service Companies.

Nayyar, D. 1996, *Economic Uberlisation in India: Analytics, Experience and Lessons,* RC. Dutt Memorial Lecture. New Delhi: Orient Longman (for Centre for Studies in Social Sciences. Calcutta).

Nayyar, D. 2001, "Macroeconomic Reforms in India: Short-term Effects and Long-run Implications", in W. Mahmud (ed.). *Adjustment and Beyond: The Reform Experience in South Asia.* Hampshire: Palgrave (in association with International Economic Association). 20-46.

Nepal, National Planning Commission. 2001, *Nepal: Country Assessment and Programme of Action for 2001-2010,* Report for the Third UN Conference on Least Developed Countries, Brussels, May 14-21.

Nepal, HMG and UNDP. 1999, "Nepal's Accession to World Trade Organization", *NEP/96/010.*

Kathmandu. Non-Aligned Movement. 1984, *Directions for Reform: The Future of the International Monetary and Financial System,* Report by a Group of Experts set up by the Chairperson of the Non-Aligned Movement.

Nouroz, H. 2001, *Protection of Indian Manufacturing: An Empirical Study.* Delhi: Macmillan

OAU/AEC. 1999, "Regional Integration as a Strategy for Enhancing the Competitiveness of African Economies", The General Secretariat of the Organisation for African Unity/African Economic Community.

OECD. 2000, Patterns of Economic Growth in OECD Countries. *Paris: Organisation for Economic* Cooperation and Development.

Ozawa, T. 1992, Foreign Direct Investment and Economic Development, Transnational Corporations. 1(1): 27-54.

Pai Panandiker, V.A. (ed.). 2000, *Problems of Governance in South Asia.* Delhi: Konark Publishers.

Pakistan, Ministry of Finance. 1999, *Economic Survey* 1998/99, Islamabad: Government of Pakistan.

Pakistan, Ministry of Finance. 2000, *Economic Survey 1999/2000,* Islamabad: Government of Pakistan.

Pakistan, Ministry of Finance. 2001, *Economic Survey 2000/01,* Islamabad: Government of Pakistan.

Panagariya, A. 1999, "Trade Policy in South Asia: Recent Liberalisation and Future Agenda", *World Economy.* 22(3). May. 353-78.

Panagariya, A. 2000, "The Millenium Round and Developing Countries: Negotiating Strategies and Areas of Benefits." *G-24 Discussion Paper Series No. 1* March 2000. New York: United Nations.

Panchamukhi. P. R. 2000, "Social Impact of Economic Reforms: A Critical Appraisal" in N. Kumar (ed.), *Indian Economy Under Reforms: An Assessment of Economic and Social Impact.* New Delhi: Bookwell (for Research and Information System for the Non-Aligned and Other Developing Countries).

Panchamukhi, V. R., N. Kumar, V. L. Rao, S. K. Mohanty, L. N. Mukherjee, and M. P. Lama, 1990, *Economic Cooperation in the*

SAARC Region, Potential Constraints and Policies. New Delhi: Interest Publications.

Panchamukhi, V. R. 1992, "South-South Cooperation in South, Southeast and East Asia: A Perspective", June. New Delhi: Research and Information System for the Non-Aligned and Other Developing Countries.

Panchamukhi, V. R., V.L. Rao and N. Kumar, 1993, *Indo-Sri Lanka Economic Cooperation, An Operational Programme.* New Delhi: Interest Publications.

Panchamukhi, V. R. 1995a, "Cooperation in South Asia", *Financial Express.* 11 October.

Panchamukhi, V. R. 1995b, "Economic Cooperation in South Asia: The Crisis of Perceptions" in *Emerging South-Asian Order: Hopes and Concerns.* Media South Asia.

Panchamukhi, V. R. 1996, *Multilateral Ageement on Investment (MAI), What Should be the Response of the Developing Countries.* Geneva: South Centre.

Panchamukhi, V. R. 1998, "Globalisation, Competition and Economic Stability", *Occasional Paper No.* 51. New Delhi: Research and Information System for the Non-Aligned and Other Developing Countries.

Panchamukhi, V.R. 2000a, "World Trade Organization and India-Challenges and Perspectives", *Discussion Paper No. 1.* New Delhi: Research and Information System for the Non-Aligned and Other Developing Countries.

Panchamukhi, V. R. 2000b, *Indian Classical Thoughts on Economic Development and Management*, Vidyaratna Sri R.S. Panchamukhi Indological Research Centre. New Delhi: Bookwell Publications.

Panchamukhi, V.R. 2001, "Lessons from the National Experience of India in Mobilizing Domestic and External Resources for Economic Development", *Asia-Pacific Development Journal.* 8(1). June. 69-99.

Panchamukhi, V. R., and R. U. Das, 1997, "Subregional Development in SAARC: Cooperation is the Key". *Business Line (The Hindu),* April 22, New Delhi.

Panchamukhi, V. R., and R. U. Das. 1998, "Rules of Origin under different Trading Schemes: Some Conceptual and Policy Issues". New Delhi: Research and Information System for the Non-Aligned and Other Developing Countries.

Panchamukhi, V. R., and R. U. Das, 2001, "Conceptual and Policy Issues in Rules of Origin: Implications for SAPTA and SAFTA", *South Asia Economic Journal.* 2(2), July-December.

Pandey, V. 1998, "Future Power Lies in Mega Projects, SAARC Grid". *The Sunday Times of India,* December, 27.

Pigato, M. C. Farah, K. Itakura, K. Jim, W. Martin, K. Murrcll, and T.G. Srinivasaa 1997, *South Asia's Integration into the World Economy.* Washington D.C: The World Bank.

Porter, M.E., 1990, *The Competitive Advantage of Nations,* New York: The Free Press.

Poudyal, S. R. (ed.), 1999, *Trends in Nepalese Economy: Foreign Trade and Investment.* Kathmandu: Centre for Policy Studies.

Proctor, A. and D. Shah. 1994, A Strategy for Promoting Foreign Direct Investment in Pakistan: The Role of Government, Paper prepared for the Pakistan Private Sector Development Conference, Lahore University of Management Sciences (LUMS), 12-13, April.

Radelet, S and J. D, Sachs., 1998, "The East Asian Financial Crisis: Diagnosis, Remedies, Prospects", *Brooking Paper on Economic Activity,* 1: 1-55.

Raghavan, C. 1998, "Current Reports, UNCTAD's Trade and Development Board," *Third World Economics.* 1-15 November.

Rajyaguru, N., 1998, "South Asian Software", *The Financial Times,* 1 July.

Ramakrishnan, R. 1999, "Inspection and Maintenance of Retrofitting of In-use Vehicles", Paper presented at the SAARC Seminar on *Improving Infrastructure in the Energy, Transport and Communications Sector.* 10-11 December. New Delhi: India International Centre, Indian Council South Asian Cooperation and TERI.

Ramasamy, B. 1995, "Trade Diversion in an ASEAN Free Trade Area", *ASEAN Economic Bulletin,* Julv. 12(1), pp.

Ramesh, J. 2000, "Pipedreams to Pipelines", *India Today*. 18 September.

Rana, P.B. 1997, "Reforms in Bangladesh: A Comparative Assessment in Relation to Other South Asian Countries" in M.G. Quibria (eds.). *The Bangladesh Economy in Transition*. Delhi: Oxford University Press.

Ranganathan, V. 2000, "Keep Government out of Power," *The Economic Times*, 19 September.

Rangarajan, C. 2000, *Structural Reforms in Industry, Banking and Finance: A Case Study of India*. RIS. New Delhi and ISEAS, Singapore.

Rangarajan, C. 2001, "Leading Issues in Military Policy", *Sukhomoy Chakravarty Memorial Lecture*, New Delhi: Sukhumoy Chakravarty Memorial Trust and RIS.

Rao, C.H. H. 2001, A Viable Agriculture in the New International Trade Regime Scenario. *Lecture at National Academy of Agricultural Sciences*. New Delhi, 5 June.

Rao, G. 2000, "Unocal to lay gas pipeline from Dhaka to Delhi, AP", *The Economic Times*, 24 February.

Rao, M. et al. 1999, "Struggling with the Digital Divide". *Economic and Political Weekly*, November 20.

Rao, V. L., S. Baruah, and R. U. Das. 1997, *India's Border Trade with Select Neighbouring Countries*. New Delhi: Research and Information System for the Non-Aligned and Other Developing Countries. RBI. 2001. *Annual Report 2001*. August. Mumbai: Reserve Bank of India.

Ricupero, R. 2001, Presentations at the Seminar on Global Governance and Trade and the Way Forward held in Geneva and to the Ministerial Conference of the OECD, (Paris).

Rij al, K.1999, "Commercialisation of Renewable Energy Technologies in the Hindu Kush Himalayan Region I". Paper presented at the SAARC Seminar on *Improving Infrastructure in the Energy, Transport and Communications Sector*. 10-11 December, New Delhi: India International Centre, Indian Council for South Asian Cooperation and TERI.

Rinzim, C. 1998, Paper presented at the South Asia Energy Symposium on *Energy Policies of South Asian Nations, Towards the 21st Century*, Tokyo: Ministry of Foreign Affairs of Japan, 27 February.

RIS. 1998, *SMRC Partnership in Progress: A Visionary Agenda*. Report of the SAARC Expert Group on SAARC Tripartite Study, New Delhi: Research and Information System for the Non-Aligned and Other Developing Countries. RIS. 1999, *SMRC Survey of Development of Cooperation, 1998/99*, New Delhi: Research and Information System for the Non-Aligned and Other Developing Countries.

RIS. 2002a, *Impact of Enhancing Environmental Standards on South Asian Trade*, Report of G-77 IPGTF-RIS Project. New Delhi: Research and Information System for the Non-Aligned and Other Developing Countries, (forthcoming).

RIS. 2002b, *Financing for Development and Reform of International Financial Architecture*, New Delhi: Research and Information System for the Non-Aligned and Other Developing Countries. (forthcoming).

RIS. 2002c, *South Asian Textile and Garment Exports in Post-MFA Scenario*. New Delhi: Research and Information System for the Non-Aligned and Other Developing Countries, (forthcoming).

Rodriguez, F. and D. Rodrik. 1999, "Trade Policy and Economic Growth: A Skeptic's Guide to Cross-National vidence", *NBER Working Paper No. W7081*. April.

Rodrik, D. 2000, "How Far Will International Economic Integration Go?", *Journal of Economic Perspectives*. 14 (1), Winter, 177-186.

SAARC Secretariat. 1991, *Study on Trade, Manufactures and Services*, Kathmandu: SAARC Secretariat.

SAARC Secretariat. 1998, SAARC Vision Beyond the Year 2000: Report of the SAARC Group of Eminent Persons. Delhi, Shipra Publications.

SAARC Secretariat. 1999a, *SAARC Newsletter*, 10(3 and 4), March and April.

SAARC Secretariat. 1999b. *SAARC Newsletter* 10 (5 and 6), May and June.

SAARC Secretariat, 1999c, *SAARC Newsletter*, 10 (7 and 8), July and August.

SAARC Secretariat. 1999d, *SAARC Newsletter,* 10 (9 and 10), September and October.

SAARC Secretariat. 2000, *Regional Economic Cooperation: Initiatives within the SAARC Region.* SAARC Secretariat.

Seeta Prabhu, K. and S. V. lyer. 2001, "Public Provision of Social Security: The Challenge in South Asia". *South Asia Economic Journal.* 2(1). January-June. 31-66.

Sahai. S. 2000, "GATTI WTO and the TRIPs Agreement: A South Asian Perspective. *South Asia Economic Journal.* 1 (2). September. 25-41.

Samaratunga, R. H. S., S Jayasuirya and D. Prentice. 2001, "Impact ofAPEC on South Asia: An Analysis of Trade Potential". *South Asia Economic Journal.* 2(2), July-December.

Sen, A. 2000, "Natural Gas Imports into South Asia: A Study in International Relations", *Energy Policy,* 28 (11), September.

Sender. H. 2000a, "Building the New India", *Far Eastern Economic Review,* 20 July.

Sender, H. 2000b, "Second Take-off, *Far Eastern Economic Review,* 20 July.

Severino, R.C. 1999, *ASEAN Rises to Challenge,* Jakarta: The ASEAN Secretariat.

Shand, R.1998, "Economic Liberalisation in South Asia: Performance and Prospects," *Occasional Paper No. 54.* New Delhi: Research and Information System for the Non-Aligned and Other Developing Countries.

Sharma, K. 2000, "Liberalization and Structural Change: Evidence from Nepalese Manufacturing", *Center Discussion Paper No.* 812, Economic Growth Center, Connecticut: Yale University.

Shetty, V. 1999, "South Asian Software and Services", *Financial Times Survey,* 2 June. Simon, L. D. 1999. "The Death of the Productivity Paradox: The Digital Explosion in the US Economy", WTO Information Technology Symposium, Geneva, WTO. 16 July.

Singh, K. 1998, *A Citizen's Guide to the Globalisation of Finance.* New Delhi: Madhyam Books.

Singh, K. 2000, *Taming Global Financial Flows: A Citizen's Guide,* New Delhi: Madhyam Books.

Sinha-Roy, S. 2001, "Post-reforms Export Growth in India: An Exploratory Analysis". *Discussion Paper No.* 13. New Delhi: Research and Information System for the Non-Aligned and Other Developing Countries.

Sobhan, R. 1999, "The East Asian Model in the Light of Contemporary Experience in Dubey, M. and N. *Jetly (ed.).* South Asia and Its Eastern Neighbours, Building a Relationship in the 21st Century. *New* Delhi: Friedrich Ebert Stiftung. 40-57.

Sobhan, R. 2000, "Problems of Governance in South Asia: An Overview", in Pai Panandiker, V.A. (ed.). *Problems of Governance in South Asia.* Delhi: Konark Publishers. 1-26.

SPDC. 1999, *Social Development in Pakistan: Annual Review.* Social Policy and Development Centre. Karachi: Oxford University Press.

Srinivasan, T.N. 1999, "Poverty and Refonns in India." Paper presented on the Conference on Reforms, organised by NBER and NCAER. 14-15 December. Rajasthan: Neemrana Fort Resort.

Srivastava, V and Sengupta, R. 2000, *Meeting India's Petroleum Requirements, Demand Projections 2001-02 and 200607.* New Delhi: NCAER.

Stiglitz. J. 1998, *Prebisch Lecture* at the UNCTAD, Geneva in October 1998, as excerpted in *Third World Economics,* 115 November.

Taylor, P. 1998, "South Asian *Software". Financial Times,* 1 July.

Taylor, P. 1999, "South Asian Software and Services". *Financial Times Survey,* June 2.

TERI. 1997, *Report on the Viability and Feasibility of Energy Cooperation in the SAARC Region.* New Delhi: Tata Energy Research Institute.

Thant, M., Tang, M., and Kakazu, H., (eds.). 1995, *Growth Triangles in Asia: A New Approach to Regional Economic Cooperation.* Manila: Asian Development Bank.

The Asian Age. 1999, "Lanka Tea Team to Apprise Pak on SAARC Success," 12 May.

The Economic Times. 2000, "Textile Ministry for control on acrylic yam imports from Nepal." 26 December.

The Economist. 2000, "The Trade Agenda: A Different, New World Order", 11 November.

The Economist. 2001, "China, America and Japan: The Uneasy Triangle", 17 March.

The Economist 2001, "From Bad to Worse.Down on the Farms". 3 March.

The Financial Express. 2000. Dhaka, 8 February. 1.

The Hindu. 1999. "SAFT A, Investment Pact to Get SAARC Nod." 19 March.

The Hindustan Times. 2000, "India well placed to meet IT manpower demand till 2008".

The Hindustan Times. 2000, "Indo-Bangla Meet to Sort Out Details of Bus Service, 18 May.

The Times of India. 1999, "SAARC Charter for Social Sectors Mooted", 19 March.

Tinberten, J. 1954, *International Economic Integration*. Amsterdam: Elsevier.

Tongia, R and Arunachalam, V.S. 1999, "Natural Gas Imports by South Asia, Pipelines or Pipedreams?" *Economic and Political Weekly*, 1 May.

Uchikawa, S. (ed.). 2000, "Pakistan's Crisis: Political and Economic Analysis". *IDE Spot Survey*. March. Tokyo: Institute of Development Economies and Jetro.

UN. 1994, *Energy Statistics Yearbook*, 1994, New York; United Nations.

UN. 2000, *Report of the Secretary-General. Towards a stable international financial system, responsive to the challenges of development, especially in the developing countries*. New York: United Nations.

UN. 2001, Report of the Secretary-General to the Preparatory Committee for the Highlevel International Intergovernmental Event on Financing for Development. New York: United Nations.

UNCTAD. 1995, *World Investment Report* 1995: *Transnational Corporations and Competitiveness*. New York: United Nations.

UNCTAD. 1997, *World Investment Report* 1997: New York: United Nations.

UNCT AD. 1998a, *The Least Developed Countries* 1998 *Report*, New York and Geneva.

UNCTAD. 1998b, *World Investment Report* 1998: New York: United Nations.

UNCTAD. 1999a, *Trade and Development Report* 1999, New York: United Nations.

UNCTAD. 1999b, *World Investment Report* 1999: New York: United Nations.

UNCTAD. 1999c, *Analysis of Experiences in Selected Services Sectors.* TD/B/COM. I/28. Geneva: UNCTAD. UNCTAD. 1999A, *"Assessment of Trade in Services of Developing Countries: Summary of Findings"*, Background note by the UNCTAD Secretariat-UNCTAD/ ITCD/TSB/7. Geneva. UNCTAD.

UNCTAD. 199ge, *The Developmental Impact of Trade Liberalization Under GATS,*. Infonnal Note by the Secretariat, Job No. 27 48/Rev. l.

UNCTAD. 2000a, *Trade and Development Report 2000,* New York: United Nations.

UNCTAD. 2000b, *World Investment Report 2000:* New York: United Nations.

UNCT AD. 2000c, *Handbook of Statistics.* New York: United Nations.'

UNCTAD. 2000d, *World Investment Directory 2000, Vol. VTI Asia and Pacific, Parts I and H,* New York: United Nations.

UNCTAD. 200 la, *Trade and Development Report 2001,* New York: United Nations.

UNCTAD.2001b, *World Economic Situation and Prospects 2001.* Department of Economic and Social Affairs and United Nations Conference on Trade and Development. New York: United Nations.

UNCTAD.2001c, *World Investment Report 2001.* New York: United Nations.

UNCTAD/WTO. 2000, *The Post-Uruguay Round Tariff Environment for Developing Country Exports: Tariff Peaks andTariff Escalation.* TD/B/COM. 1/14/RE V.I. January 28. Geneva: UNCTAD.

UNDESA. 1998, *World Economic and Social Sun'ey* 1998: *Trends and Policies in the World Economy,* Department of Economic and Social Affairs, New York: United Nations.

UNDP. 1997, *Human Development Report* 1997, New York: Oxford University Press.

UNDP. 1998, *Human Development Report* 1998. New Delhi: Oxford University Press.

UNDP. 1999a, *Human Development Report* 1999, New York: Oxford University Press.

UNDP. 1999b, *Nepal's Accession to World Trade Organization.* Project Status Review Preparatory Assistance Phase (January 1997 to June 1999), Kathmandu: Ministry of Commerce and United Nations Development Programme, Nepal. Nep/96/010.

UNDP. 2000, *Human Development Report 2000.* New York: Oxford Univesity Press.

UNDP. 2001, *Human Development Report 2001.* New York: Oxford Univesity Press.

UNICEF, *The State of the World's Children 2001.* New York: United Nations.

UNIDO. 2001, *International Yearbook of Industrial Statistics 2001.* Vienna: United Nations.

US, Energy Information Administration. 1999, *International Energy Outlook* 1999. Washington, D.C.: Department of Energy.

Uswatte-Aratchi, G. 2001, "Slow Adjustment and Faster Growth in Sri Lanka," in *W. Mahmud (ed.), Adjustment and Beyond: The Reform Experience in Sout!; Asia, IEA Conference Volume No.* 128. Hampshire: Palgrave (in association with International Economic Association). 7486.

Vaidya, R.A. 1998, Paper presented at the South Asia Energy Symposium on *Energy Policies of South Asian Nations, Towards the 21st Century,* Tokyo, Ministry of Foreign Affairs of Japan, 27 February.

Vajpayee, A.B. 2001, "Inaugural Speech", *Sustcdnable Development Summit.* New Delhi, 7 February.

Viner, 1. 1950, *The Customs Union Issue.* London: Carnegie Endowment for International Peace.

Wade. R. 2001, "Global Inequality: Winners and Losers". *The Economist.* 28 April. 73-5.

Waqif, A.A. 1991, Regional Cooperation in Industry and Energy, Prospects/or South Asia. New Delhi: Sage.

Wamer, A. M. 2000, Global Competitiveness Report: Trial Survey Sri Lanka, 2000. Colombo: ORG-MARG Smart.

Watal, J. 2001, *Intellectual Property Rights: In the WTO and Developing Countries,* Delhi: Oxford University Press.

Weerakoon, D. and J. Wijayasiri. 2000, "WTO and the Textile and Garment Sector: Implications for Sri Lanka", *South Asia Economic Journal.* 2(1). September. 95111.

Wheeler, D. and A. Mody. 1992, "International Investment Location Decisions: The Case of US Firms", Journal of International Economics. *33: 57-76.*

Wickramasinghe, U. 2000, "Services Trade as a New Frontier in South Asia: Is the Optimism Warranted?" *South Asia Economic Journal.* 1 (2). September. 123.

Wickramasinghe, U. 2001, "Energy for Economic devel-pment in South Asia: Present Status, Future Requirements, and Potential for Regional Cooperation". *South Asia Economic Journal. 2* (2), July-December. Wignaraja, P, "Towards a Traditional Strategy for Good Governance and Poverty Eradication in South Asia". *South Asia Economic Journal.* 1 (I): 117-53. March.

Williamson, J. 2000, "The Role of the IMF: A Guide to the Reports", *International Capital Markets,* 20 (2 and 3). September 39-55.

World Bank. 1998, *Global Development Finance.* Washington D.C.: The World Bank.

World Bank. 1999a, *Global Economic Prospects* 1998-99. Washington D.C.: The World Bank.

World Bank. 1999b, *Foreign Direct Investment in Bangladesh: Issues of Long-run Sustcdnability,* Bangladesh, October 1999.

World Bank. 1999c, *Global Development Finance: Analysis and Summary Tables,* Washington, D.C.: The World Bank.

World Bank. 1999d, *World Development Report: Knowledge for Development Including Selected World Development Indicators 1998-99,* New York: Oxford University Press (for the World Bank).

World Bank. 2000a, *East Asia Recovery and Beyond, Washington.* D.C.: The World Bank.

World Bank. 2000b, *World Deveopment Report 1999/2000,* Washington D.C.: The World Bank.

World Bank. 2000c, *World Development Indicators, 2000,* Washington DC: The World Bank.

World Bank. 2001a, *Global Economic Prospects and the Developing Countries,* Washington, D.C.: The World Bank.

World Bank. 2001b, *Global Development Finance 2001: Building Coalitions for Effective Development Finance.* Washington D.C.: The World Bank.

World Bank. 200lc. *World Development Report 2000-2001: Attacking Poverty.* New York: Oxford University Press (for the World Bank).

World Bank. 2001d CD-ROM on *World Development Indicators. 2000/01.* Washington D.C.: The World Bank.

World Bank. 2002, Global Economic Prospects and the Developing Countries. *Washington D.C.: The*

World Bank.

WTO. 1998, Annual Report, *Geneva: World* Trade Organisation.

WTO. 1999, Guide to Uruguay Round Agreement. Geneva: World Trade Organisation.

WTO. *2000a, Annual Report.* Geneva: World Trade Organization.

WTO. 2000b, *International Trade: Trends and Statistics 2000,* Geneva: World Trade Organization.

WTO. 2001a, *WTO Services Talks Press Ahead,* WTO News: 2001'Press Releases, Press/ 217, Geneva: World Trade Organization.

WTO. 2001b, *Market Access: Unfinished Business: Post-Uruguay Round Inventory and Issues,* Special Study 6, Geneva: World Trade Organization.

Zaidi, S. A. 1999, *Issues in Pakistan's Economy.* Karachi: Oxford University Press.

Zedillo, E et al. 2001, Recommendations of the High-level Panel on Financing for Development. 22 June. New York: United Nations.

Index

M

N

O

P

Q

R

S